The American Short Story

William Peden

The American Short Story

*Front Line in the
National Defense
of Literature*

*Houghton Mifflin Company Boston
The Riverside Press Cambridge 1964*

For Miriam, with love

Parts of Chapter Two have previously appeared in Studies in Short Fiction *(Vol. I, No. 1, Fall 1963), published by Newberry College, Newberry, South Carolina. Copyright 1963 by Newberry College. Portions of Chapter Three were first printed in* Story *(Vol. 142, No. 5, Sept.– Oct. 1963). Copyright 1964 by Story Magazine, Inc.*

First Printing   w

Acknowledgments

THIS STUDY was made possible by a fellowship from the
John Simon Guggenheim Memorial Foundation and by
a sabbatical leave of absence and research professorship from
the University of Missouri; I am grateful to the Foundation
and the University for their support.

A few of these comments originally appeared in consider-
ably different form in the *New Republic*, the *New York
Times Book Review*, the *Saturday Review*, *Story*, and the
Virginia Quarterly Review; Chapters Two and Three were
published in abridged form in *Studies in Short Fiction* and
Story; all are used with permission.

It is a pleasure to thank the good friends who have aided

73508

me: Saralee Burchell for her patient help in preparing and typing the manuscript; Whit and Hallie Burnett for their comments on part of the manuscript; Ward Dorrance for his stern admonitions; Norman Macleod, who years ago nudged me out of the eighteenth century and in effect reintroduced me to contemporary American literature; my colleagues Donald Drummond and Thomas McAfee for their assistance in many ways; and finally, as always, my wife and daughters.

WILLIAM PEDEN

Columbia, Missouri

Contents

The American Short Story

1. Backgrounds and Antecedents

PARADOX has characterized the development of the short story in America. Although it is the only major literary form of essentially American origin and the only one in which American writers have always tended to excel, it has for decades been considered a parvenu, and until very recently most critics have refused to consider it as important as the more traditional forms of poetry, drama, and the novel. Its development has been closely associated with that of the American magazine, yet its highest achievements have been made during the last twenty-five years which have seen the continuing shrinking of the magazine market. The economic position of the serious short story writer in America has almost invariably been precarious, although for almost a century short fiction was the stock-in-trade of the American family magazine; in spite of this enormous periodical popularity the short story in book form has with only occasional exceptions been a dismal financial failure and for decades book publishers were reluctant to publish collections of short stories by individual authors.[1]

In the face of such deterrents, however, more and more American fiction writers of the last twenty-five years have found the short story to be the most exciting, challenging, and congenial of all contemporary literary forms. Though individual collections of short stories continue to be for the most part "lost" or "marginal" books which usually do not make much money or even pay their own way, they are no longer a publisher's taboo. Not only have more and more good American short story writers emerged since around 1940 than in any comparable time span in history, but more and more good volumes of short stories have been published during these years than ever before in America.[2]

[1] Even Edgar Allan Poe, the father of the short story and probably the most popular magazinist of his generation, had reason to lament that he was poor in a country where to be "poor was to be despised." In spite of his notoriety and the great success of his stories in the leading magazines of his day, he had difficulty getting his stories published in book form, and his *Tales of the Grotesque and Arabesque* (1840), one of the landmarks in the history of the short story, was a financial failure for which Poe received almost no financial return.

[2] For years, publishers have often been reluctant to refer to a collection of short stories by its proper generic name. Two examples out of many include the blurb from the Cardinal edition of *Tales of the South Pacific* which labels the book as "one of the greatest *novels* to come out of the war" (New York: Pocket Books, 1957), italics mine, or the dust jacket of Faulkner's *Knight's Gambit* in which the short story stigma is avoided by the careful references to a collection of six stories

No one has been able to explain satisfactorily or completely just why collections of short stories by individual authors "don't sell." Central to the problem, perhaps, is the association between the short story and American mass circulation magazines, and the phenomenal growth and popularity of the big "family" magazines from around the middle of the nineteenth century until the 1950's. In one major line of its early development, the short story became a piece of literary merchandise written to conform to the unsophisticated tastes of a rapidly expanding middle-class reading audience. Short story standards tended to be set by publishers of magazines who were anxious to please as many subscribers as possible, and to alienate or offend a minimum number of cash customers. The result was a rapid deterioration of the high standards of the first generation of American short story writers, Washington Irving, Edgar Allan Poe, and Nathaniel Hawthorne. What Poe called the "namby-pamby" quality of the leading nineteenth century ancestors of the mass circulation general and family magazines of our own era has always been a dominant characteristic of mass circulation magazine fiction.

The results of this sponsorship of competent mediocrity by the mass circulation magazines partially explain why the short story became a second-class literary citizen. For the commuter with half an hour or so to kill on his way to work or to the patient awaiting his turn in the dentist's chair, short stories were regarded as pleasant diversions or comfortable time-killers, but nothing to be taken seriously. In the days before World War II, when a big magazine like the *Saturday Evening Post* could be bought for a nickel and short sto-

---

as "a new *book* by America's foremost novelist" and "his new *book* in six sections" (New York: Random House, 1949), italics mine.

ries frequently appeared in the newspapers, a short story was
thought of as something to read casually and toss aside, but
not "good" enough to pay folding money for, particularly by
the individual who purchases a book only occasionally or
who joins book clubs primarily for their status value or because of snob appeal. Such reader-buyer apathy, indifference, or resistance made the book publication of short stories
an increasingly hazardous publishing enterprise. Book publishers, particularly in the inflationary period of spiraling editorial, production, and distribution costs which followed
World War II, were forced to concentrate on at least an occasional best seller or book club choice, and the short story,
perhaps more than ever before, became confined within an
ever-tightening circle of cause and effect.

This sequence of cause and effect ran somewhat as fol-
lows. Short story collections by individual authors don't sell.
Therefore most publishers for years were, and with reason,
very reluctant to include them on their lists. As the twentieth
century advanced, however, so much good short fiction was
being written that even the most commercially minded or
timid publisher was almost forced to bring out an occasional
volume of short stories as a "prestige" title if nothing else, or
as a means of obtaining or holding an author who might subsequently turn out a fat, good-selling novel. But the sales history of previous short story collections influenced the publisher to allocate a very small advertising appropriation to a
short story collection. The book doesn't get much space in
the major book pages; few if any potential purchasers hear
about it; even acquisition librarians don't know much about
it; the major critics don't include comments on even an outstanding collection of short stories in their supposedly "au-
thoritative" roundups of "Reading I've Liked" or "My Pre-
Christmas Favorites"; items about the short story writer are

more likely to turn up in the class notes of a college or alumni magazine than in the gossip columns; the book makes neither a critical nor a financial success; everybody concerned—the publisher, his promotions director, the editor who worked on the manuscript, and finally the author himself—is disgruntled. Because of all this, coupled with the dying of the magazine market, the short story writer, like the poet, has tended to be a more dedicated writer and more serious craftsman than the novelist. For the most part, he works alone, ignored by the multitude, wondering where the next fifth of bourbon will come from; certainly, he isn't deluded into thinking of his short stories as an easy means to recognition or financial reward. One result of all this is that almost inevitably the average published collection of short stories has been of higher quality than the average novel. This high quality in itself complicates further the already precarious economic situation. The realistic publisher knows he is more likely to lose rather than make money from a collection of stories and the average book buyer until very recently has thought of the short story—if he is aware of its existence at all—as egghead, obscure, highbrow, or arty.

Our national love of bigness-as-such also partially accounts for public indifference to the short story. As a people we have tended to admire bigness above quality, whether it be displayed in the bosoms of Hollywood heroines, automobile fins, or the year-in-year-out best sellers. As more and more of the automotive monstrosities of the fifties are finding their way to the junk piles and auto graveyards, more and more American book buyers and book readers have been gradually "discovering" the short story. Influenced by the accessibility of inexpensive paperback reprints of good collections of short stories in supermarkets, drugstores, airports, and bus stations, reader-buyer resistance has gradually been diminishing.

More and more readers are beginning to find that if the story demands somewhat more of the reader than the average novel, it gives him more in return. Further, such collections of short stories as Bernard Malamud's *The Magic Barrel,* distributed as a major book club alternate selection *after* it had won the National Book Award for fiction in 1959, or J. D. Salinger's *Nine Stories* have demonstrated to a growing audience that the adult short story, in addition to being artistically superior, can also be fun to read; as more and more American adults are exposed to more and more formal education and the general level of intelligence and sophistication continues to rise in America, the short story seems destined to become increasingly read, respected, and enjoyed.

Why the short story has not only survived but triumphed over the decline of the magazine market that cradled it, and why such diverse writers as Erskine Caldwell and William Faulkner, Katherine Anne Porter and John Cheever, Eudora Welty and John O'Hara have found it both the most challenging and most appealing of literary forms, is less ambiguous, less questionable than the failure of the form to sell in hard covers. The short story in America has always been a thing of individuality, freedom, and variety. Flexibility is its hallmark, and no other literary form is so close to the rapidly changing pulse of the times in which it is written and which in turn it reflects with vigor, variety, and verve. Over the years, the contemporary short story in America has proved itself large enough to include the sparse simplicities of Hemingway's "Indian Camp" and the more leisurely complexities of Katherine Anne Porter's "Flowering Judas." It can be a vehicle for depicting the most ardent social or moral convictions, like Nelson Algren's "A Bottle of Milk for Mother," or Irwin Shaw's "Sailor off the Bremen." It can be alive with the robust good humor of William Faulkner's "A Bear Hunt," or like Jean Stafford's "The Interior Castle" it can reek of the smell of the sickroom. It can be a fully plotted story of intense physical conflict, or a muted study in mood and atmosphere more akin to lyrical poetry than to traditional fiction. Like the stories and *nouvelles* of Henry James, it can be a quiet character study rich in psychological overtones and almost devoid of physical action, or it can be a "slice of life" closer to reportage than to what Percy Lubbock has called the "comprehensive art of fiction."

Equally important, perhaps, is the fact that the short story challenges the powers of the most demanding craftsmen and artists. Not without reason did Henry James refer to short fiction as "blest," "shapely," and "beautiful." In a very real sense the short story writer continuously feels his way along a tightrope between success and failure. To change the metaphor, he is like a surgeon performing an operation or a quarterback directing a football team. He must be in command of the situation at all times and in all places. Within the limited boundaries of the short story there is little or no room for lapses, false moves, irrelevancies, or technical mistakes. Although the short story in recent years has tended to be increasingly leisurely and discursive, the effect of short fiction continues to rely heavily upon compression, economy, and an unerring sense of selectivity. Unlike the novelist, the short story writer cannot explore the bypaths of a situation or ponder the intricacies of a character. He must constantly discipline his subject matter to the demands of a preconceived effect. He must be thoughtful human being and literary artist, entertainer and technician. The novelist can be digressive and discursive, careless here and slovenly there, yet still create a good novel. With the short story writer, one false move or single significant lapse is likely to result in failure.

At the same time that the short story demands as much or more of the serious writer as any other literary genre, it continues to be the most accessible form in which the comparative beginner can develop his talent and explore the extent and nature of his ability. The time and energy required to write a good first novel can sometimes be fatal; there is no way of ascertaining how many potentially able fiction writers have been crushed by "risking all" on a novel before they are ready for the task. A young writer can recover, however, from the shocks and disappointments that accompany the beginner's efforts. Thus it is that the short story remains the particular province of the young writer, the proving ground, as it were, between apprenticeship and mastery.[3]

Whether written by novice or master, the short story is particularly compatible with the temper and temperament of our age. The fragmented nature of individual and national life in our times makes it virtually impossible for most writers to consider grappling with the fundamental verities which engaged the great nineteenth century fictional masters from Dickens and Thackeray through Flaubert, Dostoevsky, and Tolstoi to Hardy and Conrad. Revolutions in personal ethics and public morality, undreamed of social and economic complexities, the explosion of anxiety, tension, and neurosis, bewildering and increasingly horrifying scientific miracles, have all resulted in the questioning of Browning's comfortable assumption that all's right with the world.[4] The

[3] Whit and Hallie Burnett have stated the matter aptly: "Short story writers are the first line of the national defense of literature. They are the young. It is with the small arms of the short story they face the world . . . rarely, in this country, does one find a . . . [major writer] who has not put in his years first with the short story." (Editors' Note, *Story, the Magazine of the Short Story in Book Form; Number Two* [New York: A. A. Wyn, 1952], p. ix.)

[4] The prevailing tone of the recent American short story has been somber, and except for Washington Irving's warmhearted and rainbow-tinted fictional excursions into the American past, our major short

short story has become the literary mirror for reflecting an
age in which the new tends to be obsolete by tomorrow, in
which only change seems permanent and ultimate destruction perhaps the only reality; in which old values, old mores,
old ideas are re-evaluated in terms of next week's headlines.
The short story, brief, elliptical, and unwinking, tends to ask
questions rather than to suggest answers, to show rather
than attempt to solve. Unlike the traditional novelists, the
short story writer usually does not bring his powers to bear on
the larger questions of where are we going, why are we here,
what is man's relation to his society, to his world. Rather, the

---

story writers have from the beginnings tended to depict the dark rather
than the light. Some of the reasons for this are historical; others are
suggestive, perhaps, of some recurring element in the national consciousness of the American artist. Poe, for example, turned early to
themes of violence, horror, and the abnormal, primarily as a hard-
headed professional writer influenced by the success of Gothic fiction
of British and European periodicals. Yet there is little question that
something deep in his morbid and psychotic nature responded to
Gothic themes and subjects. To the standard machinery of ruined cas-
tles, subterranean dungeons, demonic villains, and all the rest, Poe
brought his own almost compulsive interest in abnormal behavior and
the terrors of soul and spirit. He took the refuse of Gothic nonsense
and in his best work transformed it into art. Hawthorne at approximately the same time shared Poe's interest in the strange, the unusual,
and in the dark workings of the human mind; all his major stories present somber and disturbing insights into the human predicament. To
such beginnings naturalism added "scientific" weight to the concept of
man at the mercy of uncontrollable and indifferent natural forces. Similarly, Freudian psychology and psychoanalysis contributed clinical
documentation to the fictional depiction of personal deterioration and
decay which Poe and Hawthorne had found so compelling. There is a
direct line of descent from Poe and Hawthorne to the bleak vignettes
of Ambrose Bierce and the unwinking stories of Giovanni Verga or
Chekhov to Joyce, Anderson, and Hemingway. After that, the deluge!

short story writer focuses his attention, swiftly and clearly, on one facet of man's experience. He illuminates briefly one dark corner or depicts succinctly one aspect of a character's experience, and then passes on.[5]

As such, the short story writer is creating the dominant and characteristic literary form of the post–World War II years. More and more, the short story occupies a contemporary position comparable to that of drama in the Elizabethan Age, the essay during the period of Addison and Steele, romantic poetry in the early decades of the nineteenth century, and the novel during the Victorian era. It seems increasingly probable that future generations of historians of American literature will find in the short story, rather than the novel or the drama and poetry, the major literary contribution of recent years.[6]

[5] Compare V. S. Pritchett's "In a nervous and reckless age which is overwhelmed by enormous experience, we have inevitably formed the habit of seeing . . . in fragments rather than as a solid mass . . . and, because of this, the brief, quickly moving, epigrammatic, allusive habit of the short story usually seems to me a more natural form for our story-telling than the novel." (Preface, *The Sailor, Sense of Humour, and Other Stories* [New York: A. A. Knopf, 1956], p. v.)
[6] Some of the ideas in this chapter I have discussed previously: in the Introduction to *29 Stories* (Boston: Houghton Mifflin, 1960), pp. viii–x; in "The Tightrope Writers," *Virginia Quarterly Review* (Summer 1956), pp. 470–71; in "A Thing of Variety and Bounce," *New York Times Book Review* (Sept. 20, 1959), p. 4; in the Introduction to *Modern Short Stories from Story Magazine* (New York: Grossett & Dunlap, Universal Library Edition, 1960) pp. 4–5; and elsewhere.

2. Publishers, Publishing, and the Recent American Short Story

T HE ANTECEDENTS of the recent or "new" American short story have been discussed in such detail in recent years that no detailed discussion is needed here. Among its ancestors are the stories of Gogol, Henry James, Chekhov, Joyce, and Sherwood Anderson. *Dubliners* (1914), and *Winesburg, Ohio,* published five years later, are towering landmarks and seminal forces in its development. The new story in America was essentially a post–World War I development, forged in the restless, disillusioned years following Versailles. After the high turn-of-the-century achievements of such masters as Henry James and James Joyce, the short story in

America had become vulgarized, commercialized, and over-popularized. The new story was a reaction against and a breakaway from unrealistic, contrived, sentimentalized, and mechanically plotted short fiction. The imitators of the imitators of Kipling and O. Henry, for example, had tended to reduce the short story to a form of literary garbage and bilge-water which was far removed from reality and for the most part unconcerned with truth or artistry; the new story writers once again turned to human experience as the major subject for their fiction. They rejected the romantic excesses, the trick endings, and the formularized conflict-complication-climax improbabilities of the journalist-fictioneers. They restored to the short story a dignity and artistry which for the most part had been lacking since the best work of Hawthorne and Poe. Like Anderson, they admired simplicity in form and language; they strove for truth as they saw it; they were increasingly motivated by the "hunger to see beneath the surface of lives." [1]

[1] Sherwood Anderson, Dedication, *Winesburg, Ohio. A Group of Tales of Ohio Small-Town Life* (New York: Modern Library, n.d.).

For Frank O'Connor, the modern short story begins with Gogol. Without his "The Overcoat," O'Connor states, "scores of stories by Turgenev, by Maupassant, by Chekhov, by Sherwood Anderson and James Joyce could never have been written" (*The Lonely Voice. A Study of the Short Story* [Cleveland: World, 1963], p. 16). Austin McGiffert Wright analyzes in sometimes exhausting detail the basic changes in direction and method of the American short story after World War I, in terms of the short fiction of Anderson, Faulkner, Fitzgerald, Hemingway, and Katherine Anne Porter (*The American Short Story in the Twenties* [Chicago: Univ. of Chicago Press, 1961]). Ray B. West comments on its historical development in Chapters One and Two of *The Short Story in America, 1900–1950* (Chicago: Henry Regnery, 1952). Perfunctory but useful summaries appear in Mary Jane Wing, *Studies in the American Short Story* (Chapel Hill: Univ. of North Carolina Library Extension Publication, XXII, 1, October 1956) and

The mass circulation magazine, as I have mentioned in the preceding chapter, can claim little credit for encouraging the new short story; to the contrary. Today, with such mass circulation general or family magazines as *Collier's* only a memory, and with the *Saturday Evening Post* and the remaining reputable "big flats" or "big slicks" apparently fighting for their lives, it is painful, though necessary, to recall the shallowness and mediocrity of much of the short fiction which was published in these and similar magazines.

Technical adroitness has always characterized the slick story; with few exceptions the fiction in the mass circulation magazines was the work of skilled and disciplined professionals. The big slicks catered to the demands of a huge audience; it has been estimated that during the late forties and early fifties, *Collier's,* the *Saturday Evening Post,* and *This Week* reached a combined weekly audience of upwards of sixty million readers. Such periodicals rewarded their authors generously. During a period when many small magazines of high quality could pay their contributors little or nothing, the big slicks conducted recruiting raids as zealously as did the talent scouts for Hollywood and bigtime

---

Danforth Ross, *The American Short Story* (Minneapolis: Univ. of Minnesota Pamphlets on American Writers, 1961). Chester E. Eisinger's *Fiction of the Forties* (Chicago: Univ. of Chicago Press, 1963) is primarily concerned with the novelists of the decade; it also contains perceptive comments on some of the short fiction of the period. Two bibliographies of criticism and analysis are useful but surprisingly incomplete: Jarvis A. Thurston, O. B. Emerson, Carl Hartman, Elizabeth V. Wright, *Short Fiction Criticism. A Checklist of Interpretation Since 1925 of Stories and Novelettes (American, British, Continental) 1800–1958* (Denver: Alan Swallow, 1960); Warren S. Walker, *Twentieth Century Short Story Explication. Interpretations, 1900–1960 Inclusive, of Short Fiction Since 1800* (Hamden, Conn.: The Shoe String Press, 1961).

football. More than one editor of a little or quality magazine had reason to lament the loss of one of his discoveries, and more than one critic commented that the gap between the large circulation and small circulation magazines amounted to a disaster to American literature.[2] For despite its technical skill, its external variety, and its rapid pace, the average mass circulation magazine story was little more than an adroitly manufactured or elaborately disguised refugee from the shallow and meretricious world of the pulp magazine.

The slick story masked its endless variations upon the boy-meets-girl theme beneath the camouflage of "fine writing" or the paraphernalia of costume and period; occasionally it attempted to adorn its intrinsic shabbiness with the vestments of "social awareness." Though preoccupied with the upper classes or the unusual or the romantic, and though restricted by many taboos, it made a pretense of contemporaneity; during the war years, for example, hundreds of formula stories in the big slicks simply put their heroes in uniform and proceeded with business as usual.

But beneath the costume of the lady of quality, the grimy rags of the street urchin or the faltering accents of the social climber were usually apparent. This perpetual striving to masquerade as something it was not is perhaps the most objectionable characteristic of the slick-paper story. Though the major characters in one annual anthology—selected from the pages of the *Saturday Evening Post*—include a cook who doubles for a dictator, a red merry-go-round horse, and a young man from Kansas who loudly proclaims "I'm just like a million other guys," the actors in most mass circulation fiction are as stereotyped as those of the old class-B horse operas or their equivalents in today's television series: heroes tend to

[2] Paul Engle, Introduction, *Prize Stories, 1957* (New York: Doubleday, 1957), p. 11.

be as lean and muscular as those of the pulps, heroines conventionally attractive and aching for love, villains sinister and dark.

The male lead of one story from the collection already noted is a man of "brown leanness" who looks "sorely weary." Another is "tall, gaunt, blond . . . in rather loose-fitting but well-made dinner clothes." The heroine of one story is "tall and blond and expensively beautiful"; another is a "tall, fine-figured girl . . . with the west wind in the tumble of her yellow hair" and a "little nose all wrinkling with her lovely smiling"; still another is a "trim person . . . [who] harbored a vaguest hint of crushed musk roses" and owns "violet eyes and a mischievous nose, and cheeks that could easily fall into merry curves"; yet another is a "slim, pretty young woman with large blue eyes" and lips "eager for his kiss."

And so it goes. There is not much dignity, little humor, and less truth in the antics of these impostors. Their spurious struggles are less meaningful than last year's minor league box scores. They are tormented almost beyond endurance by their ingenious creators—they are pickled in a deepfreeze for six months to escape paying inheritance taxes; their beloved old tavern is in danger of being torn down; their pet pigeons are set upon by savage hawks. But their problems, be they trivial or tremendous, are usually solved in the last paragraphs. A philandering artist, we are led to believe, will be faithful to his rich wife; a benevolent bus driver and his kindly mother, whimsically addressed as "Muscles," will live happily ever after with the "The Pup," a beautiful but homeless young woman whom they have rescued from despair; and a muscular minister will eventually make a suitable mate for his gay hoyden of a wife. After the hugger-mugger of complication and intrigue and suspense which constitutes the heart of such stories, the characters steal away into sweet-smelling lands of comfortable, never-to-be-again-complicated human relationships conducted in split-level homes with paneled rumpus rooms and chrome-and-plastic kitchens where merry housewives perform their duties in beautifully gowned ease, and the electric garbage disposal unit never falters or fails.[3]

Considerable difference of opinion exists as to why such responsible magazines as *Collier's* or the *Post* consistently published such mediocre fiction. The presence of this mediocrity has been explained and sometimes defended in realistic terms: like any other big-business operation, the mass circulation magazine must operate at a profit. This is certainly understandable, but its corollary—that for a mass circulation magazine to operate in the black its fiction must take no chances, offend nobody, experiment with nothing not virtually guaranteed to succeed—is open to question. More than one fiction editor of a big slick has proclaimed orally or in print that he wished to improve the quality of his magazine's fiction, but was continuously influenced by reader action to adhere to the level of competent mediocrity which a childlike or unsophisticated "composite reader" demanded. For example, any violation of a basic taboo, it has been said, could cause an immediate drop of thousands of newsstand purchases and a flood of cancelled subscriptions. Some contributors to the fiction pages of the big slicks have placed much of the blame on their editors; after all, they say, with more candor than dignity, one has to eat. Other critics have laid the responsibility directly on the doorstep of "someone upstairs," while some have singled out the big advertisers as

[3] All of the preceding examples and quotations are taken from *The Saturday Evening Post Stories, 1952* (New York: Random House, 1952); the generalizations, however, are applicable to almost any comparable magazine, or to almost any year in the late forties or fifties.

the major villain, stating that the only real function of the mass circulation magazines was to provide advertising space for big business which kept the magazine in the black and directly or indirectly influenced editorial policy.[4]

Whatever its reasons, the insipidity of most family magazine fiction is an unfortunate chapter in the history of American literature. The magnitude of this failure is underscored by even a superficial examination of the two annual anthologies of superior stories originally published in American magazines and periodicals, *The Best American Short Stories* and the *O. Henry Award Prize Stories*. The first *Best* collection was published in 1916 under the editorship of Edward J. O'Brien. Growing out of Mr. O'Brien's dedicated belief "in the democratic future of the American short story as something by no means ephemeral," subsequent *Best* collections have more than justified Mr. O'Brien's hopes that these annual anthologies "may do something toward disengaging the honest good from the meretricious mass of writing with which it is mingled." [5] An enthusiastic and indefatigable editor, as well as a sound and perceptive critic, Mr. O'Brien continued editing the *Best* collections until his death in 1941. Since then the series has been edited without interruption by Martha Foley, assisted in recent years by David Burnett.

[4] Consumer reaction in recent years to the occasional intelligent motion picture or television script, the phenomenal success of inexpensive LP records of high quality, the explosion in the quality paperback field, the improvement of the selections distributed by the two major book clubs, or the surprisingly large sale of recent books like Katherine Anne Porter's *Ship of Fools* or J. D. Salinger's *Raise High the Roof Beam, Carpenters* indicate that an increasingly large percentage of the American fiction-reading public was ready for something more demanding and more rewarding than the drivel of the big magazines.
[5] Edward J. O'Brien, Introduction, *The Best Short Stories of 1915* (Boston: Small, Maynard, 1916), pp. 6, 11.

In 1918 several members of the Society of Arts and Sciences of New York, many of whom had been associated with O. Henry during his Manhattan days, met to establish a "memorial to the author who had transmuted realistic New York into romantic Bagdad-by-the-Subway." [6] Out of this meeting grew the O. Henry Memorial Award Prize Stories, the first collection of which was published in 1921 under the editorship of Blanche Colton Williams. Like Mr. O'Brien, Miss Williams and the other judges who made the selections for this first volume sought "originality, excellence in characterization, skill in organization of plot, [and] power in moving emotions," [7] and like O'Brien, she was a knowledgeable and dedicated editor. She was followed, successively, by Harry Hansen (1933–1940), Herschel Brickell (1941–1952), Paul Engle (1955–1959), no volumes appearing in 1953 and 1954, following Mr. Brickell's death, Mary Stegner (1960), and Richard Poirier (1961–).

The short story is at once the most personal and most varied of contemporary literary forms, and to cull a handful of superior stories from the annual quagmire of American periodical fiction is a staggering task. Inevitably one editor's preference may be another's anathema. Miss Foley, for example, seemed for some years to be overpartial to stories and authors from the metropolitan New York area, and appeared surprisingly indifferent to the work of some distinguished Southern writers. Mr. Brickell, on the other hand, was partial to Southern fiction, and occasionally went to quite unnecessary justifications of his admiration for such writers as Eudora Welty or William Faulkner. Paul Engle's first

---

[6] Blanche Colton Williams, Introduction, *O. Henry Memorial Award Prize Stories, 1919* (Garden City: Doubleday, Page, 1921), p. vii.
[7] Harry Hansen, Introduction, *First-Prize Stories from the O. Henry Memorial Awards, 1919–1954* (Garden City: Hanover House, 1954), p. xi.

O. Henry collection contained so many selections by writers in one way or another associated with the State University of Iowa as to evoke cries of protest from some critics, and the first *O. Henry* volume edited by Richard Poirier seemed dismayingly pretentious. In face of the formidable duties involved in preparing such collections, however, certain selections or omissions, editorial timidity or preciosity, and personal preference or antipathy, inevitably evoked heated and sometimes violent disagreement. Whatever their errors of judgment or sins of omission and commission, these editors have performed their duties with awareness, responsibility, and dignity. The role of these collections in stimulating the growth of short fiction in America has been considerable. Readers and writers, specialists and laymen alike, are permanently in their debt.

From 1940 through 1963, 625 short stories were anthologized in twenty-three *Best* collections. From 1940 through 1963, with no volumes being published in 1953 or 1954, the *O. Henry* editors reprinted 412 stories. Only thirty-nine, or approximately 6.2 percent, of the *Best* stories originally appeared in the big slicks. Of these eleven were taken from the *Saturday Evening Post,* eight from *Good Housekeeping,* five from *Cosmopolitan,* four from *Today's Woman,* two from the *Ladies' Home Journal,* two from *Woman's Day,* two from *Collier's,* two from *McCall's,* two from *Redbook,* and one from *Playboy.* Of the *O. Henry* selections, only fifteen, or less than 4 percent, were from the same group of mass circulation magazines, with the *Post* again leading the way with eight anthologized stories, followed by *Collier's* with three, *McCall's* with two, and *Redbook* with two.

The shocking nature of these figures is heightened when one recalls that one extremely small circulation, low-budget periodical, *Story,* in one year, 1940, contributed eight stories to the *Best* anthology, the same number that the *Saturday*

Evening Post, with its high fees to writers and its vast circulation, contributed to the entire series of *O. Henry* collections from 1940 through 1963.

In the absence or near absence, then, of anything resembling either encouragement or sponsorship from the big magazines, the American short story writer who grappled with concepts larger than what the teenage mentality and morality were concerned with during a particular season had to find an outlet for his work elsewhere. Of the varied "little" or "advance-guard" magazines, quality monthlies, university-sponsored quarterlies, and similarly difficult-to-classify publications, probably the two most significant and influential were *The New Yorker* and *Story.* Though entirely different in concept, character, economic resources, and circulation, *The New Yorker* and *Story* shared a common interest in originality, intelligence, and literary excellence. Each in its own way played a vital role in the renaissance of American short fiction.

The first number of *The New Yorker* appeared on February 21, 1925, but it was not until somewhat later that the fictional type labeled the *"New Yorker* short story" developed. The battle for freedom of form and idea had, of course, been fought and to a considerable degree won before Harold Ross conceived his idea of a weekly magazine not edited for the little old lady in Dubuque. *The New Yorker* did not, as has sometimes been said, produce a revolution in the contemporary short story. Rather, it stimulated and helped influence the direction of a literary form which had already asserted its independence and begun to establish its own sense of direction. As the magazine prospered, its influence inevitably deepened and widened; circulation, for example, rose from 77,500 in 1929 to 125,000 in 1934, a period which saw the death of several small magazines with valid claims to literary excellence. By the middle of the thirties, *The New Yorker* had won considerable snob appeal, as well as prestige honestly and honorably earned. More and more talented writers appeared in its pages; among other factors, indeed a primary factor, the magazine paid its contributors well during a period of depression and halting economic recovery when many of the quarterlies and similar magazines were reduced to rewarding their authors with cigarette or beer money, or in more than a few cases with no cash payment of any sort. In the pages of *The New Yorker* appeared Sherwood Anderson and Kay Boyle, Dorothy Canfield and John Cheever, William March and John O'Hara, Jean Stafford and James Thurber, E. B. White and John Updike, and many other fiction writers whose work is sufficiently varied as to reject, once and for all, the popular misconception of a magic formula known as the "New Yorker story."[8]

Differences of opinion concerning the fiction which appears in *The New Yorker* are varied and violent; they range from a recent hymn of praise in the *New York Times Book Review*[9] to James Purdy's contention that the "worst influence [on the short story] in America today is the *New Yorker*"[10] or James Laughlin's acid statement that "if you read all their stories every week for a year you'd begin to

[8] Some of the material in this paragraph originally appeared in my "Esthetics of the Short Story," *Saturday Review* (April 11, 1953), p. 43.
[9] Arthur Mizener, "The Voice is Quiet, the Eye is Sharp," *New York Times Book Review* (Dec. 18, 1960), p. 1. Robert Gutwillig is equally aware of the magazine's contribution but less extravagant in his review of John O'Hara's *The Cape Cod Lighter* (*New York Times Book Review* [Nov. 25, 1962], p. 16).
[10] James Purdy, letter to William Peden, April 20, 1963.

think that most of them were written by the same person us-
ing different names." [11]

Mr. Laughlin is overstating the case, but he has placed the
shaft deftly in the Achilles heel of the magazine. Similarity
of technique, subject matter, and tone have characterized a
considerable amount of *New Yorker* fiction, from the dreary
procession of self-consciously sophisticated vignettes, the
truculently plotless slice-of-life pieces of the thirties and
early forties, the continuing bland and often smug preoccupation with middle-class manners and mores among the
pseudo-intellectuals, to the spate of too-too sensitive or
embarrassingly nostalgic narrative sketches and "remember
when" fictional essays on what life was like before "things
became so awful" and when Grandmama's cook really knew
how to turn out a good *crêpe Suzette* or a lobster Newburg.

Less than praiseworthy, too, is *The New Yorker*'s policy of
seizing upon an occasional talented author and wrapping
him (at times almost smothering him) in the sweet-scented
lamb's wool of a special contract which in effect, unless he
has unusual integrity or a substantial private income or
both, tends to make him a comfortable chattel. Equally unfortunate has been an apparent tendency to favor inferior
stories by a favored group of authors, including members of
the magazine's staff, at the expense of more talented "unknowns" or "outsiders," and a fondness for glossy technique
at the expense of originality or "different" subject matter.

In spite of all this, the real and continuing contribution of
The New Yorker is indisputable. Over the long haul, issue
in and issue out, it has published more good fiction than any
other magazine in America.[12]

[11] James Laughlin, Foreword, *Fifteen by Three* (Norfolk, Conn.: New
Directions, 1957), p. v.
[12] The merit of *New Yorker* fiction is indicated by the frequency with
which its stories appear in the *Best* and *O. Henry* anthologies, by the

Story, on the other hand, was from its beginnings in Vienna in 1931 a small-budget, low circulation magazine avowedly interested in "short stories of significance by no matter whom and coming from no matter where," a policy which launched the magazine on its precarious and, eventually, distinguished career. Its founders, Whit Burnett and Martha Foley, were co-editors for ten years until 1941, when Martha Foley left the magazine to edit the *Best* annual anthologies after the death of Edward O'Brien.

In 1942, Hallie Southgate Burnett became co-editor with Whit Burnett. Prior to this, *Story* had always had an "angel," although from 1942 until 1948 the Burnetts continued it without such financial support, financing the magazine mainly from books published under the Story Press imprint. In 1948 it suspended publication for two years, resuming as a hard cover semi-annual for four volumes, and in 1960, after another hiatus, it was reactivated as a quarterly through the assistance of co-editor Richard Wathen and the University of Missouri. In 1962 it acquired the sponsorship of the University of Cincinnati and the Reader's Digest Foundation (for annual college story contests), and regained its original rhythm as a bi-monthly. Characterized by its senior editor as a "quixotic attempt . . . to rescue the creative American short story from what looked, at that time, like possible extinction," [13] *Story* consistently emphasized quality and originality rather than conformity or big name appeal, and its

---

number of good volumes of short fiction originally published in its pages, and by the stories in three selections from its pages: *Short Stories from The New Yorker* [1930–1940]; *55 Stories from The New Yorker* [1940–1950]; *Stories from The New Yorker 1950–1960*, all published by Simon and Schuster, 1940, 1949, and 1960.

[13] Whit Burnett, Foreword, *The Story Pocket Book* (New York: Pocket Books, 1944), n.p.

open-door policy of no taboos of subject matter, technique, or length encouraged many unknowns who subsequently achieved literary distinction. It has been said that this "consistent policy of sponsoring genuine talent and important innovation" is the magazine's most important contribution.[14] In its pages such diverse authors as William Saroyan, Jesse Stuart, Ludwig Bemelmans, J. D. Salinger, Norman Mailer, Truman Capote, John Knowles, Tennessee Williams,[15] and Joseph Heller were first published. With few exceptions most of the major writers of recent years have been among its contributors, and more stories from its pages were anthologized during the thirties and forties than from any other American magazine with the exception of *The New Yorker*.[16]

Many other magazines and periodicals have contributed to the recent growth and vigor of the short story in America. The *Atlantic Monthly* and *Harper's Magazine* have for decades highlighted the monthly magazines which more or less consistently published adult short fiction; both these magazines have maintained this high quality during the years since 1940. *Harper's Bazaar* and *Mademoiselle*, among the more specialized large circulation magazines, have pub-

[14] Frederick J. Hoffman, Charles Allen, Carolyn F. Ulrich, "Story," *The Little Magazine; A History and a Bibliography* (Princeton: Princeton Univ. Press, 1946), p. 303.
[15] With "The Field of Blue Children," first story to carry the name Tennessee Williams; "The Vengeance of Nitrocris," however, appeared in *Weird Tales* prior to this, when Williams was sixteen years old.
[16] The *London Times Literary Supplement* labeled *Story* the "most distinguished short story magazine in the world," and many anthologies have come from its pages, including *Story: the Fiction of the Forties*, ed. Whit Burnett and Hallie Burnett (New York: Dutton, 1949) and *Firsts of the Famous*, ed. Whit Burnett (New York: Ballantine Books, 1962).

lished many good stories; so has, to a lesser degree, *Esquire,* in spite of a fluctuating and sometimes incomprehensible editorial attitude towards its fiction.

It is a truism that American literature is filled with the histories of talented fiction writers whose early literary careers were a series of publishers' rejections, disappointments, and frustrations. Almost without exception, even our major short story writers from Poe and Hawthorne to Anderson, Hemingway, and Faulkner have had reason to lament the scarcity of magazines willing to publish fiction which was new, controversial, experimental, or "different." From a serious author's point of view there have never been enough magazines to provide media for the particular kind of story he is interested in writing, and there probably never will be. Probably at no other period in our history, however, has the need for adult magazines been more acute than since 1940. Here again we are faced with a paradox.

America has been producing more and more talented writers during the last two decades than at any comparable period in its history. But World War II and the inflation of the late forties and fifties ended the epoch when a handful of dedicated author-editors could produce an entire issue of a "little magazine" for a fraction of the cost that a magazine like the *Post* was paying one of its favorite contributors for a single story. At the same time the mass entertainment media of big slicks, Hollywood, and television were draining away what is the lifeblood of any significant literary movement or renaissance, the young, talented, uncompromising writer without a market for his work.

The burden and the responsibility and the challenge, then, fell upon a varied group of little magazines, quality monthlies, quarterlies, advance-guard or experimental periodicals of one sort or other, and miscellaneous publications includ-

ing a few hardbound or paperback books. The most important of these have been the college or university-associated
quarterlies, ranging from journals of opinion which publish
an extremely limited number of short stories a year, to magazines specifically devoted to fiction, criticism, poetry, and
in some cases the visual arts.

In the former category, the *Virginia Quarterly Review*
and the *Yale Review* are outstanding, although the small
amount of space in these magazines allocated to fiction has
caused more than one critic to lament.[17] Among the specifically literary magazines, outstanding service has been rendered by the editors and sponsors (by sponsors I am referring to those who pay the bills; with very few exceptions none
of these publications even begins to make its own way finan-
cially) of *Accent*, the *Antioch Review*, *Epoch*, the *Kenyon
Review*, *Prairie Schooner*, *New Mexico Quarterly*, the *Sewanee Review*, the *University of Kansas City Review*, and
many others. Comparable in intent, though not associated
with a specific American educational institution, are magazines like the *Hudson Review*, or experiments in book form
like *discovery*, *New Campus Writing*, or Scribner's short-
lived *Short Stories*.[18]

[17] "Surely, Yale University and the University of Virginia might do
more," Edward J. O'Brien wrote in 1940. "Each has a distinguished
review . . . but neither . . . prints more than two or three American
stories a year." (Introduction, *The Best Short Stories 1940* [Boston:
Houghton Mifflin, 1940], p. xiv.) The *Virginia Quarterly*'s current
sponsorship of the Emily Clark Balch short story and poetry awards
would, I am sure, gratify Mr. O'Brien, as would the fact that the magazine now publishes eight or nine stories a year.

[18] I have made no attempt to include in this list all the praiseworthy
magazines which in one way or other have encouraged the development of the short story in recent years; rather, I have tried to indicate
some of the major periodicals and suggest the nature of the different

Such publications, as I have already indicated, are hazardous undertakings. For the most part, such magazines have extemely small circulations, so small as to amaze anyone unfamiliar with the field (one of the more distinguished quarterlies survived for years with a paid subscriber list of fewer than five hundred), and it has been recently estimated that the combined circulation of the several dozen little magazines in America today is less than a third that of the *Atlantic Monthly*.[19] Because of their limited circulation, such magazines are unable to obtain any substantial revenue from advertising, and cannot pay their editors or contributors more than token payments, let alone meet the magazine's production and distribution expenses. As a result, publisher, editor, and author tend to be confined within an Iron Maiden of economic stress: such publications can survive only if they receive some kind of continuing subsidy, from the academic institution with which they are associated, or from an outside source such as a publisher, a private donor, a foundation, or some similar benefactor.

The publishing landscape of the last two decades is littered with the remains of such magazines. Among the bleaching bones of scores of lesser-known victims are those of such distinguished publications as *Accent* and the *Southern Review*. The need for such magazines is even greater to-

---

types of magazines in the field. Many of these and similar publications are discussed in the definitive study of the little magazine movement by Hoffman, Allen, and Ulrich, *The Little Magazine*. Unfortunately no comparable study exists for the years following the publication of this admirable book in 1946. Among the best of several recent appraisals of the services such magazines have rendered is George P. Elliott's "Merits of 'Little Magazines,'" *St. Louis Post-Dispatch* (Dec. 2, 1962), Christmas Book Section, p. 1.
[19] Elliott, "Merits of 'Little Magazines.'"

day than when these and many other excellent publications foundered and expired. Walt Whitman's comment that for a country to have great poets there must be great audiences too, must be amended to read that to have great writers and great audiences there must first of all be publications to encourage that which is new, good of its kind, meaningful, and vital. Without a flourishing periodical market, a vigorous American literature is an anachronism and an impossibility.

3. The Period in Retrospect

IT IS DIFFICULT and hazardous to generalize about a period which includes such varied short story writers as Nelson Algren, Louis Auchincloss, Warren Beck, Stephen Vincent Benét, Paul Bowles, Kay Boyle, Ray Bradbury, Erskine Caldwell, Hortense Calisher, Truman Capote, John Cheever, Walter VanTilburg Clark, Ward Dorrance, Elizabeth Enright, James T. Farrell, William Faulkner, Mavis Gallant, Martha Gellhorn, Caroline Gordon, William Goyen, Nancy Hale, William Humphrey, Charles Jackson, Shirley Jackson, Christopher and Oliver La Farge, Andrew Lytle, Carson McCullers, Bernard Malamud, William March, Flannery

O'Connor, John O'Hara, Tillie Olsen, Katherine Anne Porter, J. F. Powers, James Purdy, Philip Roth, J. D. Salinger, William Saroyan, Irwin Shaw, Jean Stafford, Wallace Stegner, Jesse Stuart, Peter Taylor, Robert Penn Warren, Jerome Weidman, Eudora Welty, Christine Weston, Tennessee Williams, and John Updike.[1] One conclusion at least is inescapable: Since the early forties, the American short story has come completely of age.

During the last two decades more and more American short story writers have been creating more skillfully, more artistically, more meaningfully, than ever before in our national history. It is no exaggeration to suggest that there have been dozens of American fiction writers since 1940 who, technically speaking, are much better novelists than James Fenimore Cooper ever was, or Hawthorne and Melville occasionally were. And there are scores who can write better short stories—again speaking in terms of technical achievement—than Hawthorne and Poe sometimes did. Even our very young writers—the Truman Capote of *A Tree of Night*, for example, published when the author was only twenty-five, or Philip Roth whose National Book Award–winning *Goodbye, Columbus* came out when he was twenty-six, or John Updike whose first collection of short stories, *The Same Door*, was published when he was twenty-seven—display dazzling virtuosity and technical adroitness. Comparison of any of the *Best* or *O. Henry* annual collections of

[1] Although such established writers as Erskine Caldwell and John Steinbeck continued to write short stories during the forties and fifties, their major contributions to the field were made before 1940. Hemingway, with Faulkner the greatest American short story writer of the twentieth century, virtually abandoned the form by the end of the thirties. Faulkner and Katherine Anne Porter made their major contributions prior to 1940, though each continued to work with distinction with the short story during the decades included in this study.

American short stories since 1940 with those of the twenties, for example, is like comparing, in terms of technical skill and functional achievement, a crystal receiving set of the twenties with one of today's radios.

The reasons underlying this marked increase in technical skill and artistic achievement are many, varied, and often difficult to assess. Unquestionably, however, the influence of the American college and university is a dominant factor. A half century ago, young writers like Jack London, Richard Harding Davis, Stephen Crane, and O. Henry served their apprenticeships and developed their talents during careers as practicing journalists; today, the college classroom or the faculty study have for the most part replaced Hawthorne's "solitary chamber" or the newsroom as incubators for creative growth and development. Even most of our smaller and less experimental educational institutions now offer some work in "creative writing" or boast of a writer-in-residence, and more and more young writers begin to produce seriously while they are undergraduates, are first published in college or university literary magazines, and with increasing frequency combine the dual roles of writer and teacher. Long considered a pariah, gate-crasher, or at best a parvenu, the "teacher of writing" has become accepted within the framework of the American college and university.

The older generation of such writer-teachers included the likes of Robert Frost, William Faulkner, and Katherine Anne Porter; essentially they were visitors occupying honorary positions or advisory chairs and did comparatively little if any formal teaching. Important as their roles have been, they were for the most part outside the movement to which they brought honor and dignity. More basically a part of higher education in America, however, are today's writer-teachers who are full-fledged members of their academic communities and whose duties include the "teaching of writing." (The phrase is unfortunate: obviously no one can *teach* anyone to write or to paint or to compose music, or to run the mile in four minutes or throw the discus two hundred feet, and few, if any, respectable writer-teachers make any such claims. The instructor conducting a class in the writing of poetry or the short story, however, *can* offer editorial advice; he can aid in stimulating whatever talent his students may possess; he can help shorten the apprentice period, and help provide a climate of mutual respect and encouragement; he can weed out the utterly untalented but earnest student whose energies should be directed elsewhere. Only the occasional fraud or deadbeat within the profession presumes to offer his students more than this.)

The roster of such writer-teachers is impressive and remarkably diverse; it includes or has included Robert Penn Warren, Cleanth Brooks, Caroline Gordon, Hudson Strode, Wallace Stegner, Mark Schorer, Walter VanTilburg Clark, Philip Roth, George P. Elliott, George Garrett, Bernard Malamud, Thomas Williams, Andrew Lytle, Alan Swallow, Howard Nemerov, Allan Seager, Paul Engle, James B. Hall, Jean Stafford, Peter Taylor, Mary McCarthy, Reynolds Price, and Sylvia Berkman.

The presence of these and many, many other able teacher-writers suggests that for the next few years at least their influence will be basically good. It remains to be seen, however, whether this situation will eventually have a good or a bad effect on American literature. The movement, if it can be called such, already shows signs of provincialism and commercialism; today some universities sponsor so-called "Writers' Conferences" which have little more to do with writing than a homecoming football weekend has to do with higher education. Similarly, some university-sponsored resident writing programs seem more interested in luring big-name writers to their campuses than in hiring experienced teachers, and are more intent on publicity than in attending to the business of teaching and learning. Such activities subject the less flamboyant university writing programs to suspicion and, eventually, ridicule. Criticisms of academic writing programs and the writer-as-teacher are becoming more and more frequent; characteristic is E. M. Forster's petulant comment that a certain writer's short stories are "completely free from the slickness that comes from attending courses in Creative Literature." [2]

At one time or other most of the shortcomings of contemporary fiction have been laid at the doorstep of the writer-teacher. These defects include the painful artiness of a considerable amount of the smaller or advance-guard magazine fiction; preoccupation with technique at the expense of substance and story; the love of the crutch of symbolism and the contact lenses of multiple meanings; the pretentiousness which often stalks like Madeline Usher through the pages of some little magazines; the fondness for obscurity, dilettantism, and over-intellectuality; and, perhaps most damning of all, what has been called its increasing tendency toward uniformity of subject matter and method.[3]

[2] E. M. Forster, Introduction, Donald Windham, *The Warm Country* (New York: Scribner, 1961), p. 9. If colleges and universities recruit their writing students as their athletic departments recruit athletes, the movement will have begun to outlive its usefulness; it is unsound, however, to damn the many because of the excesses or absurdities of the few. Two quite different appraisals of the role of the writer within the ivied walls are found in John W. Aldridge's "The Writer in the University," *In Search of Heresy; American Literature in an Age of Conformity* (New York: McGraw-Hill, 1956), pp. 35–69, and William Van O'Connor's "The Writer and the University," *The Grotesque: An American Genre, and Other Essays* (Carbondale: Southern Illinois Univ. Press, 1962), pp. 177–92.

[3] All these comments are valid to a degree (whether or not the writer-

Whatever the pros and cons, writing programs in American colleges and universities are here to stay—at least for a while. Whatever their drawbacks, the universities seem to provide the most satisfactory emotional and economic climate for the serious writer who is not blessed with a private income or a wealthy spouse or patron. Whether he aids or endangers his own creative career and the young talent entrusted to him is more debatable than is the assumption that some of the technical skill which characterizes today's serious short fiction can be attributed to his presence and example.

If technical skill, artistic virtuosity, and mechanical adroitness were the major factors in the production of significant fiction, the years since 1940 would be golden ones indeed. The palpable achievement of the recent American short story demonstrates for the thousandth time, however, that technique must be a means to an end, not an end in itself. Technique not employed in the service of some end

---

teacher is responsible for them), but they fail to take into account the overall vigor, variety, depth, and independence of the recent short story in America. In his *Strangers to This Ground; Cultural Diversity in Contemporary American Writing* (Dallas: Southern Methodist Univ. Press, 1961), W. M. Frohock persuasively argues that many of the frequent criticisms of the alleged "conformity" of recent American fiction are misleading, and that the "cultural situation in the United States at this moment is infinitely more complex than a reading of books like *The Lonely Crowd* has led us to think" (p. 173). Frohock's conclusions concerning the seeming paradox of "variety amid monotony" are particularly applicable to the short story since 1940. The bulk of the literature of any period—be it Elizabethan or Stuart poetry, neo-classical essay or Victorian novel—is uniform, to be sure, but within this framework the short story since 1940 or thereabouts is remarkable in its diversity—diversity of mood, setting, subject matter, characters, technique.

larger and greater than itself, usually becomes futile, meaningless, decadent, or destructive. The indispensable element
in a short story (indeed in any work of art, though the generalization is peculiarly applicable to the short story in which
superficial social awareness and technical skill sometimes
masquerade as more immediately important than they really
are) is the presence of a consciousness larger than that of any
of the characters of a particular story, an illumination above
and beyond plot, setting, theme, and incident—what Allen
Tate and Caroline Gordon have called the presence of a
"superior . . . intelligence playing over the incidents" of a
piece of fiction.[4]

This is the ultimate, the indispensable, dimension of fiction. It is this which gives meaning to the marriage of character and incident which constitutes the heart of a short story.
Something seldom or never part of an author's deliberate
attempt, it is his way of seeing the world, his way of distilling
his experience as a human being in a world of constantly
shifting values, ideas, and mores. It is this largeness of vision which makes possible some kind of moral identification
between the author and the adult reader, and makes the
reading of a piece of fiction a rewarding human experience.
Without it, any story, no matter how skillfully or cunningly
contrived, tends to be little more than a momentary diversion
or an achievement in technical logistics. Oversimplifying a
complex problem, one might say that to be a significant
author a writer must first of all be a significant human being,
must know deeply, feel deeply, be aware deeply. This is what
makes Hawthorne and Melville and Twain and Anderson
greater writers than Bret Harte or Richard Harding Davis;

[4] Allen Tate and Caroline Gordon (eds.), *The House of Fiction: An
Anthology of the Short Story with Commentary* (New York: Scribner,
1950), p. 193.

this is why the fiction of J. D. Salinger and Eudora Welty is more significant than that of Mickey Spillane or Vina Delmar.

Such illumination, such awareness of the survival of the significance of the human experience even on the threshold of annihilation, is the product of many factors: the writer's belief in himself and in the worthiness of his art, his respect for the world he is in the process of creating and for its inhabitants, his need to communicate his own individual view of the world, whether that view be essentially tragic or comic, skeptical or optimistic, exalted or debased. Henry James's much-quoted comment that the "figures in any picture, the agents in any drama, are interesting only in proportion as they feel their respective situations" can be extended to suggest that the events in a work of fiction are meaningful to a reader in proportion to their meaningfulness to the participants of the story, and by further extension in proportion to their meaningfulness to their creator. This involves, in a special kind of way, "old-fashioned" concepts of loyalty and commitment, of belief in the significance of the universal human experience and dilemma, and of obligation between author, his fictional world, and his audience. For the reader to become involved in a work of fiction, to care, to share, to be moved, the creator must be at once involved but detached, committed but withdrawn, identified with his materials yet above and beyond them. It is this sense of commitment which provides a common denominator among the very different worlds of such writers as Flannery O'Connor and Bernard Malamud, between James Purdy and Katherine Anne Porter, paradoxically enough during a period characterized by an ever-increasing emphasis upon the usual, and by the emergence of the non-hero, or the anti-hero.

It is a truism that the arts reflect the age in which they are created. Although literary fashions frequently change with as little apparent rational reason as do women's fashions, literary changes for the most part are caused by—and reflect and, in turn, influence directly or indirectly—changes in the contemporary social, moral, political, and ethical climate. Of no artistic form is this more true than the short story, the most strictly contemporary, the most sensitive to change of all twentieth century imaginative arts.

The towering, overwhelming, inescapable facts of the last quarter century have been the War and the Bomb. The revelations of human depravity, for example, which resulted in the civilian exterminations at Dachau or Buchenwald, or the lesser but no less hideous massacres of military personnel at Katyn Wood or Salamaua and dozens of less-publicized burying grounds, forced even the most traditionally minded adult mentality to question the ultimate goodness of man and society. The Bomb, similarly, made it necessary for him, if only occasionally, to reconsider the basic Christian-democratic concept of the significance of individual effort, the importance of individual destiny, and the idea that human beings could control or influence the direction of history and their roles in it.[5] The "post-peace" years which saw no peace tended to diminish, at least for the present generation, any reasonable hopes for restoring or even revitalizing the order and stability and wholeness of the past. Matthew Arnold's brave adjuration to let Reason and the Will of God prevail became almost as anachronistic as the Tennysonian concept of man as "heir of all the ages, in the foremost files of time."

The War and the Bomb brought into sharp focus the skeptical re-evaluation of the Christian-democratic vision of life which had flowered so fully during the nineteenth century. Confronted by fragmentation and disorientation, many writ-

[5] Walter Allen comments on this succinctly in "But Somebody Should Have Something to Say," *New York Times Book Review* (Jan. 28, 1962).

ers questioned or rejected the tranquil Victorian concept of life and civilization as something essentially meaningful, orderly, and reasonable presided over by an essentially benevolent Deity.[6] In a century over which hovered enormous shadows—suffering, injustice, and meaningless waste of dignity and resources and life, and the constantly gnawing awareness of the possibility of both individual destruction and the annihilation of the past as well as the present—the outraged cries of the hurt Romantics and the literary Peter Pans mingled with the don't-give-a-damn chantings of the Beats and the gruntings of Nihilists and Existentialists whose partial to total rejection of traditional values and beliefs were in their own ways escape hatches as neatly engineered as Browning's muscular optimism or a jet pilot's seat-ejection mechanism.

Meanwhile, the man in the street was beginning to find that in rejecting the medieval devil he was becoming victimized by his many contemporary equivalents, all designed to make his existence miserable—atavistic tyrannies and archetypal woes; tension, allergies, insomnia; air pollution and dwindling or corrupted natural resources; and the presence of radioactive materials in the milk his children drank. Life and business, in short, went on pretty much as usual except for the fact that even the most somnambulistic Babbitt was occasionally aware of the dry, mirthless chuckle in the cosmic corner, or could at times sense the announcement of his own obituary in the crashing of the time barrier.

It is little wonder, then, that seriousness of purpose and somberness of tone are as characteristic of much short fiction of the forties, fifties, and early sixties as are artistry and tech-

[6] See A. Alvarez's controversial "The New Poetry, or Beyond the Gentility Principle," *The New Poetry* (London: Penguin Modern Poets, 1962).

nical skill. Long before Pearl Harbor, of course, the trend toward subdued, unsensational realism had commenced; long before Hiroshima, more and more twentieth-century short story writers shared with Verga, Chekhov, Joyce, and Anderson the realization that in the lives of "ordinary" or "non-exceptional" human beings the artist could find an unending source of fictional materials and themes. The melodrama, sensationalism, romanticism, improbability, contrivance, and surprise-or-happy-ending formulas of the past were questioned, found wanting, and for the most part rejected. Both the heroics and the mechanics of earlier short fiction became increasingly unpalatable in light of current newspaper headlines.[7]

Increasingly, the American short story was concerned with the familiar, the everyday, the non-spectacular, with the complexities underlying apparently "normal" situations. As Verga had depicted the drama in the lives of the people he observed in his corner of Sicily in the 1860's, as had Joyce in his Dublin in the 1900's and Anderson in his Winesburg, such short story writers as John Cheever, Peter Taylor, Jesse Stuart, and Hortense Calisher examined, evaluated, and created their own segment of mid–twentieth century America, finding in it all the subject matter, all the drama and all the conflict, they desired. Writers like James Michener, Eugene Burdick, or John Berry continued, of course, to owe much of their success or popularity to their use of "faraway places

[7] But it is wise to recall that, as Wilbur Daniel Steele has astutely observed, for the United States of the Golden Age the Happy Ending was "no mere catchpenny escape mechanism . . . It was solid realism. It was such matter-of-fact in the faith of then, that most men discover gold mines on grubstakes and die wealthy, as it came to be in a later faith, that most men buy utilities . . . and live unhappily ever afterward." Introduction, *O. Henry Memorial Award Prize Stories of 1943* (New York: Doubleday, Doran, 1943), p. xxii.

with strange-sounding names," but for the most part small
town, rural community, farm, suburbia, and big city replaced
Poe's torture chambers, Bret Harte's boomtowns of the Old
West, or Jack London's Klondike gold camps.[8] In our most
significant recent short fiction large-scale heroics have been
noticeably absent. The classic conflict of man against nature or the fall from grace of the superman has been replaced,
for the most part, by incidents in the life of the non-hero, the
little man whose problems are important and meaningful to
him if to no one else—John Cheever's Johnny Hake ("How
sad everything is") or Roger Angell's Halleck ("Everybody's
scared now").[9]

Most of the significant American short story writers of the
forties, fifties, and sixties avoided or eventually abandoned
the extreme positions of the never-never land Romantics on
the emotional right and the Beats and Nihilists on the literary left. In questioning or rejecting the comfortable traditional concepts of order and belief in the individual, they did
not accept the concept of man as a gaping-mouthed hyena
shivering underground while uneasily waiting to Explode
and Expire. These authors share in common, to be sure, the
realization that they and their literary creations live in a
world where somehow, somewhere along the line, the American dream of progress, decency, and order has gone awry.
For all their differences in heredity, environment, and social

[8] The popularity of the story of science fiction or fantasy, like the
success of such collections of essentially old-fashioned suspense or
surprise-ending stories as Roald Dahl's *Someone Like You* or *Kiss,
Kiss,* is probably caused in part by their break from the preponderance
of stories depicting the accustomed, the non-exceptional, the ordinary.
[9] John Cheever, "The Housebreaker of Shady Hill," *The Housebreaker
of Shady Hill and Other Stories* (New York: Harper, 1958), p. 23;
Roger Angell, "Flight Through the Dark," *The Stone Arbor and Other
Stories* (Boston: Little, Brown, 1960), p. 109.

behavior, the grotesques of James Purdy and Jean Stafford are kin not far removed from John O'Hara's suburbanites or Jerome Weidman's New Yorkers. Wanderers in a world in which the fragmentation of the present is in bleak contrast to the wholeness of the past, they are beset with loneliness, fright, sadness, or moral fatigue. "Life was essentially a matter of being done in, let down, and swindled," think some of the characters of Jean Stafford's "In the Zoo," in words echoed and re-echoed in many of the stories of the period.[10]

But the fictional world of the last decades is neither nihilistic nor meaningless, in spite of this predominance of bewilderment and hopelessness in the continuing search for identity in a society in which self-realization often seems increasingly difficult or impossible. To the contrary, author after author, story after story, reflect a slow, if often almost grudging, maturation. Life, after all, they suggest, does go on in spite of everything. The artist, in the face of great enormities, is increasingly compelled to shout his defiance, to reassert that the human experience *is* important. This almost compulsive need to create, and in creating to communicate, to reach out and touch some other human being, animates what might otherwise be a drab—if impeccably written—series of clinical case histories subtitled The Disasters of Mankind in the Middle of the Twentieth Century. On the threshold of possible destruction, the American writer has been forced into a kind of maturation which prepares him to accept without undue rancor, violence, or self-pity what most European writers and intellectuals have for years or generations taken for granted—that loneliness, despair, and tragedy are as inherent in the human situation as are their opposites; that, as W. M. Frohock has observed, "to be human at all is to live iso-

---

[10] Jean Stafford, "In the Zoo," *Stories: Jean Stafford, John Cheever, Daniel Fuchs, William Maxwell* (New York: Farrar, Straus & Cudahy, 1956), p. 26.

lated, out of complete communication and condemned to the nameless discomfort which results." [11]

In brief, American short fiction since around 1940 has tended to come of age emotionally and intellectually as well as artistically and technically. If he could not believe that tomorrow would be better, the writer was able, in many cases reluctantly, to find a kind of solace in the hope that perhaps tomorrow might not be too much worse. Human relationships are more important than philosophical speculations, much of the fiction of the period reasserts, and love more vital than nuclear physics, in spite of, perhaps to a degree because of, the threat of apocalyptic terrors. Many a writer turned his back on the Great Terrors of the forties and fifties, and began once again to cultivate his own individual garden and accept the realization that though things were bad, very bad, one is able to find cause for limited rejoicing in small private pleasures. Rather than rejecting man, many stories of the period are animated by compassion and tempered by the regret that the dream and the reality are so dissimilar. Othello's "the pity of it, Iago" is more suggestive of the tone and mood of this short fiction than his curse of "goats and monkeys!" Rather than rage or hatred or defiance, the vague, undefinable sadness of the heroine of John Cheever's "The Season of Divorce" might serve as emblem for many recent American short stories:

> Why do I cry? Why do I cry? . . . I cry because I saw an old woman cuffing a little boy on Third Avenue. . . . I can't get it out of my mind . . . I cry because my father died when I was twelve and because my mother married a man I detested. . . . I cry because I had to wear an ugly dress . . . to a party twenty years ago, and I didn't have a good time.

[11] Frohock, *Strangers to This Ground*, p. 15.

I cry because of some unkindness that I can't remember. I cry because I'm tired—because I'm tired and I can't sleep.[12]

[12] John Cheever, "The Season of Divorce," *The Enormous Radio and Other Stories* (New York: Funk & Wagnalls, 1953), pp. 193–94.

4. Jane Austens of Metropolis
and Suburbia

T HE PERCEPTIVE delineation of the everyday life of familiar segments of contemporary society, which furnished subject matter and theme for generations of English
fiction writers from Fanny Burney and Jane Austen to Thackeray and Anthony Powell, has no significant counterpart
in nineteenth-century American literature.[1] Though Henry
James and others found in the contemporary scene the major

[1] For a good recent summary and commentary, see Lionel Trilling,
"Manners, Morals, and the Novel," *Approaches to the Novel: Material
for a Poetics,* ed. Robert Scholes (San Francisco: Chandler, 1961),
pp. 231–46.

source of their short fiction, it was not until later that many of our major short story writers turned their talents to the quiet, occasionally humorous, and frequently satiric depiction of contemporary manners and mores.

Much of the most important recent American short fiction has been in this province of the usual and the non-exceptional. John Cheever, Hortense Calisher, John O'Hara, Peter Taylor, and John Updike seem to me the most important and the most representative of the many skilled and perceptive writers who have for the most part concerned themselves with incidents in the lives of ordinary men and women in familiar or immediately recognizable situations, and have created a contemporary fiction of manners characterized by skill, urbanity, and insight. Of these chroniclers of the non-exceptional, perhaps the most distinguished is John Cheever (1912–), born in Quincy, Massachusetts, educated at Thayer Academy in South Braintree, and currently living in New England. Cheever's first collection, *The Way Some People Live*, was published in 1943 when the author was in the army; it contains thirty stories and narrative sketches, most of which had originally been published in *The New Yorker*, where with very few exceptions all of his subsequent stories have appeared. Many of these early stories are brief fictional anecdotes or narrative sketches which concern a few moments or hours in the lives of a character or a group. Typical are "Summer Theatre," in which a group of amateur prima donnas display higher than average pre–opening night jitters; "Problem No. 4," in which a draftee training in South Carolina concentrates more on his wife back in New York than on his lieutenant's earnest adjurations concerning a security mission; "The Law of the Jungle," with its effective contrast between older and younger generations in pre–World War II New York; and "The Peril in the Streets," essentially a characterization in terms of a monologue delivered by an unhappy drunk in the presence of a bartender and a draftee. Longer, somewhat more ambitious stories include "Of Love: A Testimony," a restrained and melancholy depiction of a love affair doomed to failure.

Though some of these *The Way Some People Live* stories border on the trivial, the collection on the whole is an impressive one, and with very few exceptions indicates the direction the author's subsequent stories were to take. Cheever writes in a relaxed, seemingly casual but thoroughly disciplined manner; his general mood is a compound of skepticism, compassion, and wry humor; he is concerned with the complexities, tensions, and disappointments of life in a strictly contemporary world, a world of little men and women, non-heroic, non-spectacular, non-exceptional. Loneliness, perhaps the dominant mood of the short fiction of the forties, fifties, and early sixties, permeates the collection. The lament of the draft-dodging, divorced alcoholic of "The Peril in the Streets" is characteristic:

I know you hate me. It doesn't make any difference to me. I'm lonely. I'm persecuted. But I don't care. I've been lonely all my life. I know what pain is. I can take it. You think you know what pain is, but you don't. Have *you* ever seen a seagull with a broken wing? Have *you* ever seen a wild animal gnaw its leg off to get out of a steel trap? Have you—[2]

The Enormous Radio and Other Stories was published ten years later, in 1953. It is the author's best book and one of the major collections of the period. Gone are the occasional

[2] John Cheever, "The Peril in the Streets," *The Way Some People Live* (New York: Random House, 1943), p. 239.

triviality and the sometimes studied informality of the earlier stories. With only isolated exceptions, Cheever has gained complete control of his medium; he is at all times and in all places on top of his materials. The *Enormous Radio* stories concern individuals similar to the people of his first collection, though they are often older and more mature—university graduates, World War II alumni, young businessmen on the way up or slightly older ones on the way down, and their anxious, frequently harried women. The scene is contemporary, usually in or around New York City. Cheever's subject matter continues to be the usual, but his treatment of it is far from commonplace. He is concerned with the loneliness which festers beneath the façade of apparently "happy" or "successful" individuals; he suggests the potential terror or violence inherent in the metropolitan apartment-dweller's condition. Beneath the often placid, impeccably depicted surfaces of his stories there is a reservoir of excitement or unrest which is capable of erupting into violence; his well-mannered characters walk a tightrope which at any moment may break; the vast, shining city masks cruelty, injustice, and evil.

The frequently anthologized title story is characteristic, centering as it does around so commonplace a subject as a young husband's purchase of a radio as a gift to his wife. Judged by any conventional standards, Jim and Irene Westcott are "nice" people "who seem to strike that satisfactory average of income, endeavor, and respectability that is reached by the statistical reports in college alumni bulletins."[3] Married nine years and the parents of two pleasant children, they live in an apartment house near Sutton Place, attend the theater and concerts regularly, and hope to be

[3] John Cheever, "The Enormous Radio," *The Enormous Radio and Other Stories* (New York: Funk & Wagnalls, 1953), p. 169.

able to live in Westchester eventually; as Irene says, "We've always been good and decent and loving to one another." [4]

All goes well until, in the middle of a Chopin prelude, strange sounds and voices intrude; the radio has begun to penetrate the bland façade of the apartment house and Irene distinguishes discordant sounds, doorbells ringing, telephones being dialed, electric razors and Waring mixers going about their daily business. Irene is amused at first, but then the radio begins to reveal harsh and shocking details of the lives of the apartment-dwellers: "demonstrations of indigestion, carnal love, abysmal vanity . . . and despair." [5] These and subsequent revelations cause Irene to re-examine her neighbors: in the elevator she attempts to identify the secrets masked behind their "handsome, impassive faces"; at lunch with an old friend, she wonders what horrors she is hiding. Listening to the radio becomes an obsession which causes her to re-examine herself as she has been re-examining her neighbors; her search for her real self ends in disaster. Her once-amiable husband is "sick to death" of her apprehensions, and the story ends with another series of revelations:

"Why are you so Christly all of a sudden?" [Jim demands] "What's turned you overnight into a convent girl? You stole your mother's jewelry before they probated her will. You never gave your sister a cent of that money that was intended for her—not even when she needed it. . . . and where was all your piety and your virtue when you went to that abortionist? I'll never forget how cool you were. You packed your bag and went off to have that child murdered as if you were going to Nassau. [6]

[4] *Ibid.*, p. 178.
[5] *Ibid.*, p. 175.
[6] *Ibid.*, p. 180.

In terms of such characters, Cheever's sad modern comedy is played out to its inconclusive finale. With few exceptions, the people of the *Enormous Radio* stories are decent, respectable, fundamentally likeable individuals. Occasionally they win a temporary victory, like Ralph and Alice Whittemore of "The Pot of Gold"; only rarely do they become destructive and malignant, like Joan Harris of "Torch Song." [7] For the most part they exist between these two extremes, frightened and to all intents and purposes terribly alone, lost somehow in an urban no-man's land from which most of the traditional guideposts have been removed.[8]

Four of Cheever's best stories, written after *The Enormous Radio*, are included in *Stories: Jean Stafford, John Cheever, Daniel Fuchs, William Maxwell* (1956). Except for "The Bus to St. James," with its depiction of the corrosive effect on the individual of big-city mores and tensions, these stories display an extension of subject matter and theme and a more leisurely technique than most of their predecessors. The best of these is "The Day the Pig Fell Into the Well," a warm-hearted and robust recreation of the Nudd family at White-beach Camp in the Adirondacks. The story possesses a variety of character and incident more customarily associated with the novella or the novel than with the short story; over this "chronicle of small disasters" hovers a kind of Indian-summer warmth, as Cheever depicts the American equivalent of the English middle class with Galsworthian compassion

[7] A "big, handsome girl," Joan leaves the Middle West with ambitions to become a New York model; a masochist, nymphomaniac, and alcoholic, Joan thrives on sickness and disaster and well merits the cry of Jack Lorey, whom she helps destroy: "What kind of an obscenity are you that you can smell sickness and death the way you do?" ("Torch Song," p. 113.)

[8] Particularly effective are "The Season of Divorce," "The Summer Farmer," "The Superintendent," "Goodbye, My Brother."

and dislike, affection and irony.[9] Almost as good are "The National Pastime," part essay, part short story, with its nostalgic re-creation of a New England boyhood, and the prize-winning "The Country Husband," [10] one of the best of Cheever's excursions into the suburbia which was to furnish subject and theme for his next collection, *The Housebreaker of Shady Hill* (1958).

The title piece of the Shady Hill stories, with its mingling of humor, effective characterization, serious commentary, and suspense, is characteristic of the collection as a whole. Johnny Hake has a lot to be thankful for: he has a pretty wife, four loving children, a high-paying job in Manhattan, and lives in fashionable Shady Hill ("a *banlieue* and open to criticism by city planners, adventurers, and lyric poets, but if you work in the city and have children to raise, I can't think of a better place").[11] On summer nights, sitting in the garden with the children, and looking into his wife's dress as she bends over to salt the barbecuing steaks, Johnny is "thrilled." But no man in John Cheever's suburbia is happy for long. Johnny loses his job, and Shady Hill is expensive. One night, after a party, he breaks into his odious host's home, and steals nine hundred dollars. The moral bottom drops out of Johnny Hake's world—"I never knew that a man could be so miserable and that the mind could open up so many chambers

[9] *Stories: Jean Stafford, John Cheever, Daniel Fuchs, William Maxwell* (New York: Farrar, Straus & Cudahy, 1956). Some of these comments originally appeared in my "Four Cameos," *Saturday Review* (Dec. 8, 1956).

[10] "The Country Husband" was first-prize winner in *Prize Stories 1956. The O. Henry Awards*, ed. Paul Engle and Hansford Martin (New York: Doubleday, 1956), and was later made into a successful television script.

[11] "The Housebreaker of Shady Hill," *The Housebreaker of Shady Hill and Other Stories* (New York: Harper, 1958), p. 12.

and fill them with self-reproach!" [12] Like the Westcotts of
"The Enormous Radio," Johnny has opened a Pandora's box.
His own wrongdoing makes him painfully aware of the evil
and corruption around him. He seeks a scapegoat—his father, his mother, things as they are, Shady Hill—knowing
all the time that he is deluding himself. Eventually, he finds
a solution which, if pat and over-contrived, illustrates the
seriousness of purpose which characterizes much of Cheever's
stories: "There were ways out of my trouble," he concludes,
"if I cared to make use of them. I was not trapped. I was
here on earth because I chose to be. . . . It is not, as somebody once wrote, the smell of corn bread that calls us back
from death; it is the lights and signs of love and friendship." [13]

Except for the sadistic organization man of the merciless
"The Five-forty-eight," most of Mr. Cheever's non-heroes are
essentially amiable men: onetime track star Cash Bentley,
forty, who provides the climax for many a Saturday night
Shady Hill party by hurdling sofas, tables, and firescreen;[14]
Francis Weed, who becomes infatuated with the Weed's
babysitter but eventually, at the advice of a psychiatrist,
finds solace through woodwork;[15] Will Pym, whose only sin
was marrying a flirtatious woman considerably younger than
himself;[16] and Charles Flint, "fugitive from the suburbs of all

[12] *Ibid.*, p. 12
[13] *Ibid.*, p. 29. Similarly, Charles Flint's decision to stop running away
from things and to be a man rather than a self-indulgent child, in
"The Trouble of Marcie Flint": "I know that I will go back. . . . I
will see my children grow and take up their lives, and I will gentle
Marcie—sweet Marcie, dear Marcie, Marcie my love. I will shelter
her with the curve of my body from all the harms of the dark"
(p. 185).
[14] "O Youth and Beauty!"
[15] "The Country Husband."
[16] "Just Tell Me Who It Was."

large cities" [17] whose plea, written in his journal aboard ship, suggests the real villain, or scapegoat, of Cheever's world, Shady Hill itself, with its culture vultures, its meaningless activity, its joyless parties and meaningless love skirmishes, its pretentiousness and unending striving for status.

> God preserve me . . . from women who dress like *toreros* to go to the supermarket, and from cowhide dispatch cases, and from flannels and gabardines. Preserve me from word games and adulterers, from basset hounds and swimming pools and frozen canapés and Bloody Marys and smugness and syringa bushes and P.T.A. meetings.[18]

Like Johnny Hake or Charles Flint, some of these non-heroic protagonists win a partial victory through love, or by demonstrating a kind of courage or integrity; very rarely are they destroyed, like Cash Bentley; for the most part they see things through, they muddle along, a little balder, a bit more short of breath, somewhat sadder today than they were yesterday. Sorrow and disappointment pervade the book: sadness for the loss of youth and love, for the gradual dimming of the dreams of the past, and for the nagging awareness of entrapment in an often comfortable present built upon extremely flimsy moral foundation. Usually this is implicit within the narrative framework of character and incident; only rarely does Cheever indulge in the commentary of the misunderstood child of "The Sorrows of Gin", "the pitiful corruption of the adult world; how crude and frail it was, like a piece of worn burlap, patched with stupidities and mistakes, useless and ugly." [19]

[17] "The Trouble of Marcie Flint," p. 165.
[18] *Ibid.*, p. 165.
[19] "The Sorrows of Gin," p. 101.

Cheever's most recent collection, *Some People, Places, and Things That Will Not Appear in My Next Novel* (1961), contains some stories such as "The Death of Justina" or "Boy in Rome," which are among his best work, and even the slightest pieces display Cheever's hallmarks of urbanity, wit, intelligence, and technical adroitness. As a whole, however, the book is a definite letdown, fatigued and written in an over-casual manner which at its most objectionable is almost an imitation—at times, indeed, almost a parody—of Cheever's earlier work. "A Miscellany of Characters That Will Not Appear" is a moving manifesto and declaration of intent, as much essay as short story. Among the clichés and bromides of character and incident which Cheever wishes to see eliminated from fiction—his own and that of his contemporaries —are "all scornful descriptions of American landscapes with ruined tenements, automobile dumps, polluted rivers . . . diseased elm trees . . . unclean motels, candle-lit tearooms, and streams paved with beer cans,"[20] all explicit descriptions of sexual commerce, all lushes, all parts for Marlon Brando, all homosexuals, all fake artistry. Cheever's exhortation, in spite of its levity of manner, is a noble one; it would have more significance if it were not embedded in a collection which is the must uneven of Cheever's books, markedly inferior to *The Enormous Radio* and *The Housebreaker of Shady Hill*, and in some ways less impressive than *The Way Some People Live*.

Over twenty years ago Struthers Burt, the first important critic to recognize fully the extent of Cheever's talent, commented that he had only two things to fear: a "hardening into an especial style that might become an affectation, and a

[20] "A Miscellany of Characters That Will Not Appear," *Some People, Places, and Things That Will Not Appear in My Next Novel* (New York: Harper, 1961), pp. 164–65.

deliberate casualness and simplicity that might become the same."[21] Cheever's tendency toward self-imitation and his preoccupation with similar character types and situations underscore the awareness of Mr. Burt's analysis. At his best, however, Cheever is one of our most entertaining storytellers as well as one of our most perceptive and urbane commentators on the contemporary scene. A wry observer of manners and mores, he is more saddened than amused by the foibles he depicts with understanding and grace. He is the least pretentious of moralists, yet his stories present a sad and moving spectacle of loneliness, disappointment, and loss.

The most pleasant of Hortense Calisher's (1911–) stories are those concerned with incidents in the childhood of Hester Elkins who appears as child, adolescent, and adult in several of the stories in each of Miss Calisher's collections, *In the Absence of Angels* (1951), and *Tale for the Mirror* (1962). Among the best of these are "A Box of Ginger" and "The Watchers" from the first collection, and "Time, Gentlemen!" and "The Coreopsis Kid" from the second.

These excursions into the past are warmhearted without being sentimentalized, simple without ever lapsing into the trivial. Around such subjects as the death of Hester's grandmother, the child's experience on Armistice Day in New York, or her father's ritualistic breakfast, Miss Calisher has created a faithfully realized way of life and a past when there was time for pleasure, for understanding and for contemplation, and for love, "all the time in the world," as Mr. Elkins was fond of saying.[22]

[21] Struthers Burt, "John Cheever's Sense of Drama," *Saturday Review* (April 24, 1943), p. 9.
[22] Hortense Calisher, "Time, Gentlemen!" *Tale for the Mirror. A Novella and Other Stories* (Boston: Little, Brown, 1962), p. 88.

Miss Calisher recalls the world of Hester and her brother Kinny with affection and re-creates it in detail—its sights and sounds and smells, the clothes its inhabitants wore and the food they ate. It is a comfortable world of middle-class Manhattan apartment-dwellers in the first quarter of the twentieth century, a bustling active world of a large family with many cousins, uncles, and aunts "so close-knit that all its branches lived within round-the-corner call of each other." [23] Hester's father, a Virginia-born Jew who had emigrated to New York in the early 1880's, is the center of this small universe. A handsome man and a dandy in his day, a bon vivant and talker, to Hester he was "at the very least, early Edwardian." [24]

The narrator of the harrowing title story of Miss Calisher's first collection concludes that "in the absence of angels and arbiters from a world of light, men and women must take their place." [25] Unlike the stories of Hester's childhood, most of the author's other stories indicate that men and women are poor substitutes for "angels and arbiters." Almost without exception Miss Calisher depicts a society in which Hester's dream of order, wholeness, security, harmony, and happiness has been blurred almost beyond recognition or has become nightmarish.

The loss of love, the failure of a marriage, and the inability of human beings to communicate with each other are central themes in most of Miss Calisher's adult stories. On a larger scale, these failures are not just the defeats of individual men and women or of specific human relationships, but the failure of traditional social and personal values in a world

[23] *Ibid.*, p. 75.
[24] *Ibid.*
[25] "In the Absence of Angels," *In the Absence of Angels* (Boston: Little, Brown, 1951), p. 144.

so fragmented and beset by stress and tension that such traditional values have become either unrecognizable or unattainable. The young intellectual of "The Woman Who Was Everybody" is aware that she is one of the "rejected"; she tries to escape the "gray encroaching smutch of averageness" by a meaningless affair with a young technician, but knows that after the "desperate wrenches, the muffled clingings of love-making," she will still be alone and unwanted;[26] the senator's wife of "The Night Club in the Woods" tries to buy a romantic past which for her never actually existed;[27] the young man who has "moved up" from 14th Street to Sutton Place yearns for the past when love illuminated a relationship which has become meaningless;[28] the husband and wife of "Saturday Night" have become "strangers . . . too far apart even for conflict . . . sharing the terrible binding familiarities of the joint board, the joint child . . . and the graceless despair of the common bed." [29]

Miss Calisher narrates these stories of human failure and fallibility with grace, insight, and compassion. Her delineation of the nuances of a character or an incident is reminiscent of Proust in its subtlety and perception. She is, furthermore, a "superb raconteur" [30] whose delight in communicating experience is infectious. Like Cheever, she is preoccupied with essentially similar character types and situations, but within

[26] "The Woman Who Was Everybody," *In the Absence of Angels,* pp. 61–62.
[27] "The Night Club in the Woods," *Tale for the Mirror.*
[28] "The Seacoast of Bohemia," *Tale for the Mirror.*
[29] "Saturday Night," *Tale for the Mirror,* p. 108.
[30] Robert Gorham Davis, "Questions at Dawn," *New York Times Book Review* (Nov. 4, 1962), p. 5. Some of the preceding comments are from my "Out of Contrasts Two Fictional Worlds," *Virginia Quarterly Review* (Spring 1963), pp. 347–48.

these self-imposed boundaries she has created universal images.

The old Roman of contemporary fiction writers, John O'Hara (1905–) has had in effect two separate careers as a short story writer. During a long decade between the middle thirties and forties, O'Hara was probably the most prolific important writer of short fiction in American literary history; within this period he published five collections of short stories: *The Doctor's Son and Other Stories* (1935); *Files on Parade* (1939); *Pal Joey* (1940); *Pipe Night* (1945); and *Hellbox* (1947). This body of work has been so frequently commented upon as to seem to belong to another era; O'Hara's social awareness, his "toughness," his shrewd observation of manners and mores, his remarkable ear for dialogue, and his unwinking recording of "the way things were then" are almost legendary. After *Hellbox*, O'Hara abandoned the short story for another long decade until 1960 when at the age of fifty-five he discovered with delight that "in spite of aches in spine and tendons, I had an apparently inexhaustible urge to express an unlimited supply of short story ideas." [31] The result of this urge was the publication, in 1961, of *Assembly*, twenty-six stories all but three or four of which were written during the summer of 1960. This was followed in 1962 by *The Cape Cod Lighter*, twenty-three stories; yet another collection, entitled *The Hat on the Bed*, was published late in 1963.

These latest stories are among the best of O'Hara's work and display the same qualities which characterize his earlier short fiction: the penetrating and skeptical analysis of contemporary life which is Thackerayan in its delineation of

[31] John O'Hara, Foreword, *Assembly* (New York: Random House, 1961), n. p.

individual, group, and societal stupidity, and what a recent
critic has labeled society's "dull implacable hostility";[32] the
remarkable observation of speech, dress, gestures, actions,
and the thousand and one details which make his stories
seem more realistic than the columns of the newspapers of
the period; and his technical adroitness which is reminiscent
of an Archie Moore or a Stan Musial or a Pablo Casals who
has so thoroughly mastered his trade or art that even when
his reflexes have slowed down he can outperform most of his
younger contemporaries. O'Hara, in short, is a seasoned
professional who respects his work and is constantly striving
to learn more, accomplish more. If you are an author, O'Hara
comments, and not "just a writer, you keep learning all the
time." [33]

Central to the effectiveness of most of these stories is
O'Hara's remarkable knowledge of his people. He knows
them inside and out, knows what they do and what they
think; he seems, indeed, to have known them all their lives.
His preoccupation with pretentiousness, hypocrisy, arrogance, cruelty, and stupidity is as intense as it was during the
thirties and early forties when he was frequently criticized
because of lack of pity for his characters, or because he wrote
out of what seemed like intense dislike for the world he was
in the process of creating. His vision, to be sure, is extremely
limited, but not as restricted as some commentators have
indicated.[34]

[32] Lionel Trilling, Introduction, *Selected Short Stories of John O'Hara*
(New York: Modern Library, 1956), p. xiii.
[33] O'Hara, Foreword, *Assembly,* n.p.
[34] As Joseph Henry Jackson has commented, there *is* sympathy in
O'Hara, "however wryly expressed, which is why he's the writer he
is." Jackson cites as examples "The Moccasins" and "Doctor and Mrs.
Parsons," both from *Hellbox* (*San Francisco Chronicle,* [Aug. 4, 1947],
p. 16).

In occasional stories, such as "Claude Emerson, Reporter" or "The First Day," [35] for example, O'Hara's depiction of human failure is tempered with tolerance, and even affection, but for the most part his characters are cut from flawed cloth. They emerge strangely diminished, marvelous in their verisimilitude, but reduced and somehow drained both of their humanity and of their stature as human beings. It is far from accurate to say with some of O'Hara's detractors that if you've read a few of his stories you've read them all, but his interest in the same or similar character types and situations, and his depiction of essentially one aspect of human experience are his most conspicuous limitations. In spite of his very large talent and unflagging energy, his world in retrospect, with very few exceptions, becomes blurred, and its people merge into an indistinguishable mass.

Lawyer and engineer, war-rich contractor and businessman, country-club drifter, adulterer, pandering husband, wealthy homosexual, deadbeat, pimp, whore, newspaperman on the way down or saloon owner on the way up, O'Hara's non-heroes possess in common the fact that with few exceptions they have made a mess of their lives, or are on the verge of doing so. The breakdown of human relationships is his favorite theme; failure, loneliness, and boredom appear and reappear in his stories. He depicts unsparingly a continuing war of attrition between the individual and society; between the middle-aged, who constitute many of his characters and are frequently created with a depth and understanding largely absent from his earlier stories, and the young; between husband and wife and lover, if the joyless participants in O'Hara's skirmishes of the sexes can be called lovers; between parent and child. Occasionally this warfare is climaxed by physical violence including murder or homicide, as it is

[35] Both of these stories are in *The Cape Cod Lighter*.

in "In a Grove," "The Sharks," or the long story of adultery, "Justice";[36] for the most part, however, the endings of most of these stories are as studiously unresolved as they were in the author's earlier fiction.

O'Hara's segment of the world, like Thackeray's, is neither a moral place nor a merry one, but crowded, noisy, full of eating and drinking, making love and betraying love, laughing and, on the contrary, cheating, fighting, and conniving. Thackeray's parting comments upon his *Vanity Fair* might well serve as emblem for O'Hara's: "Ah, Vanitas, Vanitatum! Which of us is happy in this world? Which of us has his desire? or, having it, is satisfied?—Come, children, let us shut up the box and the puppets, for our play is played out." [37]

The short stories of Peter Taylor (1917–) concern family relationships in what the author has termed the "quiet lives" of a responsible middle class in or from Tennessee, where the author was born in the small town of Trenton, and where he spent most of his life, in Nashville and Memphis, prior to his military service from 1941 to 1946. Tennessee, Mr. Taylor has said, "was (and is) the center of the universe" to his family;[38] with few exceptions, it is the center of his fictional world. Change is the major factor in this world—the change from an agrarian to an urban society and the resulting conflicts between tradition and the present, between old pat-

[36] "In a Grove" and "The Sharks" are in *Assembly;* "Justice" is in *The Cape Cod Lighter*.
[37] Some of these comments appeared originally in my " 'Vanity Fair' Updated," *Saturday Review* (Jan. 5, 1963), p. 39. O'Hara's most recent collection, *The Hat on the Bed* (New York: Random House, 1963) appeared too late to be commented on here.
[38] Peter Taylor, *A Long Fourth and Other Stories* (New York: Harcourt, Brace, 1948), dust jacket.

terns of thought and conduct and the stresses and pressures
of contemporary life.

Although his earliest stories were written in the late thirties,
Taylor's first collection, *A Long Fourth*, was not published
until 1948. Contemporary urban middle-class Tennessee furnishes both subject matter and theme for all seven of these
stories, all of which take place in Tennessee, primarily in or
near Nashville and Memphis. All but one, "Allegiance," are
leisurely in narrative method, exploring the nuances and the
bypaths of a situation and the people involved in it with almost Jamesian thoroughness. All but one of them, "Rain in
the Heart," depict the deterioration of family relationships;
all of them center around unspectacular revelations and
crises of contemporary living; and all of them, as Robert
Penn Warren has observed, are concerned with the attrition
of old loyalties, the breakdown of old patterns of conduct,
and the collapse of old values.[39]

The title story is characteristic. "A Long Fourth" centers
around Harriett Wilson, a pretty Nashville woman "just past
fifty," and the members of her family and household—her
amiable doctor-husband "Sweetheart," Helena and Kate,
their two unmarried daughters, her son, whom she idolizes,
and two Negro servants, Mattie and her ill-smelling nephew
BT. Around Son's return to Nashville from New York prior to
being drafted, Mr. Taylor creates a moving series of quiet
and not-so-quiet character revelations. The well-bred, proud,
and genteel Mrs. Wilson explodes into violent rage when
Mattie unthinkingly compares BT's intention to work in an
airplane factory with Son's going into the Army: "Between
the moments when she even pictured Mattie's being tied and
flogged or thought of Mama's uncle who shot all his niggers
before he would free them . . . she would actually consider

[39] Robert Penn Warren, Introduction, *A Long Fourth*, p. viii.

the virtue of her own wrath." [40] Helena and Kate are shown
to be potential alcoholics, constantly nagging each other, in-
capable of giving or receiving love. Son is courteous, affable,
but completely aloof and as far removed from his family as
though he had been living on another planet, and his racial
ideas—"The people in the South cannot expect to progress
with the rest of the nation until they've forgotten their color
line" [41]—are as incomprehensible to the Wilsons as they
would be to Mattie and BT.

In *The Widows of Thornton* (1954), Taylor continues to
depict the contrast between old and new, order and change,
wholeness and fragmentation. "My idea," he has stated,
"was to write a group of stories dealing with the histories of
four or five families from a country town [Thornton, Tennes-
see] who had migrated . . . to various cities of the South
and the Midwest. . . . I wanted to present these families—
both Negro and white—living a modern urban life while continuing to be aware of their old identities and relationships." [42] Nowhere is this juxtaposition of old and new, this
awareness of old identities and relationships in the midst of
contemporary change, made more explicit than in "Their
Losses," a quiet study of contrasts in terms of three women:
two spinsters, Miss Patty and Miss Ellen, and a worldly
married woman, Cornelia Werner.

Miss Patty, who is accompanying her senile aunt to Thornton, lives in and worships the past; she laments the passing
away of the small towns between Grand Junction and Memphis which to her are symbols of a "prosperous and civilized
existence," and mourns the past glory of her family: "My

[40] Peter Taylor, "A Long Fourth," p. 140.
[41] "A Long Fourth," p. 154.
[42] Peter Taylor, *The Widows of Thornton* (New York: Harcourt,
Brace, 1954), dust jacket.

people," she tells her companions, "happened to be very
much *of* the world . . . Not of *this* world, but of *a* world
that we have seen disappear. In mourning my family, I mourn
that world's disappearance." [43] At the other extreme is Mrs.
Cornelia Weatherby Werner, like Miss Bean a native of Thornton, who had left home to marry a Memphis Jew. Cornelia
hates her mother, recently deceased, who had made her life
in Thornton miserable, yet is an alien in Memphis: "'It's a
wretched place!'" she exclaims. "'It's the most completely
snobbish place in the world. . . . They can't forgive you for
being from the country—they hate the country so, and they
can't forgive your being a Jew!'" [44] Somewhere between the
two is Miss Ellen Watkins, who is bringing home the body of
her mother for burial. A former classmate of Cornelia's, Miss
Ellen lacks the pride and arrogance of Miss Patty, and the
vigor and daring of Cornelia; she has existed in a kind of
sweet meaninglessness, with a widowed mother, a sister who
had developed melancholia, and two quiet, home-loving older
brothers who had made "little stir in the world, content to
live there in the house with Mother and Nora and me after
Father was gone." [45]

Among these three women, each in her own way suggestive of the wasted life, no rapport exists; their reunion, if it
can be called that, is as meaningless to them as Miss Ellen's
comments concerning scrambled eggs cooked with milk
which Miss Patty deliberately ignores and Cornelia hardly
hears. As the train approaches Memphis, each goes her own
way, each equally lonely and adrift, each isolated in her
pride, acquiescence, or rebellion.

Most of the people of *The Widows of Thornton* are simi-

[43] "Their Losses," pp. 20–21.
[44] *Ibid.*, p. 19.
[45] *Ibid.*, pp. 16–17.

larly unable to escape or forget the past, or to live very com-
fortably in the present. Perhaps the best story in the collection, "A Wife of Nashville," presents two of Taylor's most
memorable characters, Helen Ruth Lovell and her Negro
servant girl, Jess McGhee. When Jess suddenly leaves the
Lovell household after years of devoted service, Mr. Lovell
and the three grown Lovell sons are bewildered. Only Mrs.
Lovell can understand Jess's reasons, which in both subtle
and obvious ways grow out of a sense of loneliness and isolation which Mrs. Lovell herself experiences. Few authors
have depicted with greater understanding the gulf between
mistress and servant, between white and Negro; at the same
time, "A Wife of Nashville" presents with wry compassion
and irony two kinds of loneliness which create an enduring
kinship between mistress and servant.

In addition to Tennessee the setting of Taylor's most recent
collection of stories, *Happy Families Are All Alike* (1959),
includes Chatham—a middle-sized city "not thoroughly
Middle Western and yet not thoroughly Southern either" [46]
—and Paris, but the author's interests and preoccupations
are the same as those displayed in his two previous volumes
—the contrasts between past and present, relationships between the races, and family connections and relationships.
"A Friend and Protector," like "A Wife of Nashville," ex-
plores the relationships among members of a responsible
Tennessee family and a Negro servant and depicts with a
violence rare in Taylor's work the interacting influences of
the Negro-white relationship. The narrator of the story, an
intelligent, highly aware young man, finally realizes that the
story of Black Jesse's life and its ruin is also the story of his
aunt's "pathetically unruined life, and my uncle's too, and

[46] "The Other Times," *Happy Families Are All Alike; A Collection of
Stories* (New York: McDowell, Obolensky, 1959), pp. 7–8.

even my own," [47] and concludes that in a very real way his
family have caused Jesse's destruction because unknowingly
they were so dissatisfied with the "pale *unruin*" [48] of their
own lives.

"Promise of Rain," one of the best of the Chatham stories,
is similarly concerned with character revelation and the
growth of human awareness and self-recognition. A middle-
aged father, after frustrating months of being unable to
understand his adolescent son, witnesses an incident in which
the son is humiliated. Only then can the father look at the
world through eyes other than his own; only then can he
assess his experiences as a human being, because it is only
after such an awakening that "the world, as you have seen it
through your own eyes, will begin to tell you things about
yourself." [49]

With admirable craftsmanship, dignity, and good sense,
Taylor has produced a fictional world whose external simplicity belies its interior complexity and emotional depth.
In form his stories range from an anecdotal reminiscence of
the Veiled Prophet's Ball in St. Louis ("The Little Cousins")

---

[47] "A Friend and Protector," p. 136.
[48] *Ibid.*
[49] "Promise of Rain," p. 69. Similarly "Guests," at the conclusion of
which another middle-aged man, a Tennessee lawyer, contemplates
the body of a dead cousin, and reflects that "here is such a person as
I might have been, and I am such a one as he might have been." The
lawyer concludes that his fusing of his own identity with that of his
country cousin is the result of their sharing a common heritage—they
came both of them from the same "country," not just a geographical
place so and so many miles from Nashville, but a way of life: "the old
ways, the old life, where people had real grandfathers and real children, and where love was something that could endure the light of
day. . . . Our trouble was, Cousin Johnny, we were lost without our
old realities" (p. 206).

to a complex novella like "The Dark Walk";[50] his characters include prostitutes, domestic servants, lawyers, wide-eyed children, and a pair of college students on a spree; his range of mood embraces both the comic and the serious.

Although even his earliest fiction is impressive, Taylor's artistic development has been continuous. His narrative method has remained leisurely, and often gives the impression of oral telling which is appropriate to the frequently nostalgic or reminiscent mood of his stories. At the same time, most of his latest work is more controlled and better disciplined than its predecessors, less likely to meander down the garden path which sometimes led to the contemplation of trivia or an almost feminine concern with the subtleties of a character or a situation. As his career has progressed, Taylor has been increasingly successful with his male characters while continuing to portray with admirable insight the women who were the most successful creations of his early stories.

One of the most gentle of skeptics and civilized Jeremiahs, Taylor loves the Southern past yet is fully aware of its shortcomings. He respects the human experience yet is continuously cognizant of his characters' absurdity, their moral myopia, their stupidity, even their occasional capacity for evil and cruelty. With affection and irony he examines his characters' lives, and assesses their meanings in terms of the conflicts imposed by heredity and environment, by the conflicting values of past and present, by agrarian versus urban manners and mores, by the collision between reason and emotion.

[50] "The Little Cousins" is included in *Happy Families Are All Alike*, "The Dark Walk" in *The Widows of Thornton*. Taylor's most recent collection, *Miss Leonora When Last Seen & Fifteen Other Stories* (New York: Obolensky, 1963) appeared too late to be commented on here.

In the final analysis, Taylor's fiction is meaningful because his characters are meaningful. Most of his stories contain at least one character who becomes "finely aware" of the situations around which the action revolves, and in so doing becomes aware of himself, as the father of "Promise of Rain" becomes aware of himself. This awareness gives what Henry James has called the maximum of sense to the human experience underlying a work of fiction and it is this, primarily, which makes Taylor's carefully drawn stories so significant.

John Updike (1932–) is so talented as to be almost frightening. He has a marvelous eye and ear, curiosity, wit, sensitivity, erudition, a retentive memory, a hungry concern for the drama beneath the surface of ordinary incidents, and apparently almost boundless creative versatility and energy amply attested to in three novels, two volumes of verse, a children's book, and two collections of short stories, *The Same Door* (1959), and *Pigeon Feathers* (1962).

Most of Mr. Updike's stories are set in small-town Pennsylvania where he was born, in Shillington, and raised; in New York City where he worked for *The New Yorker;* in Massachusetts where he attended Harvard and currently lives with his wife and children. Three or four others take place in England where he studied art for a year or so. Very smooth, very relaxed and quiet, and admirably disciplined, Updike's stories are concerned with problems, reflections, and revelations in the lives of sensitive or egotistical adolescents, and equally sensitive, harried, trapped, frustrated, self-congratulatory or patronizing young people—intellectuals or pseudo-intellectuals, married couples, and parents. Most of Updike's best stories center around such ordinary situations as two former college classmates having lunch together, a young schoolteacher's difficulty with his Shakespeare class, a young married couple's return from Boston to

New York with their two infant children, a quiet evening visit of an émigré professor with two of his former students.

The larger sorrows or tragedies of life are quite naturally absent from such stories. Mr. Updike's characters live moderately comfortable lives. Depression and war exist for them, if at all, only as vague memories as remote from their actual experience as the Black Plague or the Napoleonic conquests. They live in reasonably well-furnished apartments with reasonably well-stocked bookshelves, record cabinets, and pantry shelves. They seem to know a good sherry from a poor one, and are as likely as not to read Proust or Gide before retiring.

Despite the absence of any larger catastrophes, however, most of Updike's characters are far from happy. They are introspective and easily disturbed, by matters ranging from the inconsequential to the significant. They love each other, and are good parents, but the early morning yammering of their children or the sticking of the electric toaster will sometimes set their teeth fearfully on edge. They are susceptible to insomnia, they have hard-to-shake-off colds, because of their allergies they must watch their diets, they suffer from fears of inadequacy, of being conspicuous, of being outmanned or threatened in one way or other. Doing anything in public for the first time, "carving a roast, taking communion, buying a tuxedo," makes one young man's chest "feel fragile and thin";[51] a young wife sees "homosexuals everywhere";[52] one young husband and father wishes "there were such a thing as enchantment, and he could draw, with a stick, a circle of safety" around his wife and child;[53] another, told

[51] John Updike, "Intercession," *The Same Door* (New York: Knopf, 1959), p. 194.
[52] "His Finest Hour," *The Same Door*, p. 124.
[53] "A Gift from the City," *The Same Door*, p. 163.

by a doctor he has fungus of the eyelids, immediately thinks of how beautiful his eyelashes were in his adolescence and visualizes "his face with the lids bald and the lashes lying scattered on his cheeks like insect legs";[54] still another, denied his marital pleasures, is pleased the following morning to see that his wife looks "ugly . . . wan breakfast light bleaches you blotchily, drains the goodness from your thickness, makes the bathrobe a limp stained tube flapping disconsolately, exposing sallow décolletage. The skin between your breasts a sad yellow. I feast with the coffee on your drabness." [55]

At their best, and taken singly, such stories are a triumph of the art of the usual; Updike possesses a genius for recording, as it were, the flicker of the eyelid which becomes an epiphany, and his small apartments, automobiles stuck in the snow, and mildly frustrating Sunday afternoons which make his characters reflect that "this was the sort of day when you sow and not reap" [56] are sharply observed and brilliantly recorded. At their least successful, or taken in large, sustained doses, however, they tend to be trivial rather than significant, and more dull than delightful. Particularly in *Pigeon Feathers,* after the palpable achievement and exciting talent displayed in *The Same Door,* I become bored with the triviality of such family narrative sketches as "Walter Briggs" (I'm really not interested in the word games Jack and Clare play while they're driving back from Boston); by the deftly narrated nonsense of "A. & P." which concerns nothing more significant than a checking clerk's interest in three girls in bathing suits; and by the beautifully written cliché about a

[54] "The Persistence of Desire," *Pigeon Feathers and Other Stories* (New York: Knopf, 1962), p. 19.
[55] "Wife-Wooing," *Pigeon Feathers,* p. 114.
[56] "Incest," *The Same Door,* p. 160.

young boy's disillusioning experience at a carnival, "You'll Never Know, Dear, How Much I Love You." [57]

Even more distressing, however, is the patronizing assumption of many of Updike's central characters—he appears in story after story, as Clyde Behn of "The Persistence of Desire," as Allen Dow of "Flight," as David Kern of "Packed Dirt, Churchgoing, A Dying Cat, A Traded Car"— that because something interests him it will inevitably and automatically interest his readers to a similar extent. Behn-Kern-Dow *et al.* is a younger Soames Forsyte, regarding life with head cocked to one side, nostrils faintly quivering, mouth slightly pursed, as though he were continuously aware of a decidedly unpleasant smell in the room. A self-centered egotist with slightly paranoid tendencies, he patronizes everyone he comes in contact with—a doctor who is examining his eyes, a receptionist into whose bosom he peers nearsightedly, a young sailor he gives a ride to, his family, even the country through which he travels.

Characteristic is "Flight," in which a young married writer, Allen Dow, returns to his home in Pennsylvania. "At the age of seventeen," Allen tells us, "I was poorly dressed and funny-looking, and went around thinking about myself in the third person." [58] Here begins a seemingly interminable series of reminiscences, about his mother, about *her* mother and his father and *her* father and her grandfather, and how and where his mother was educated and how she had to go to

[57] Even more disappointing than the mannerisms and repetition of these stories is the inclusion of "Archangel," a florid two-page prose poem which tends to make me wonder when Mr. Updike is going to start publishing his laundry lists; "Archangel" is the sort of bad fancy writing that all creative writing majors should jot down in their journals at three in the morning, but to rush this sort of thing into print, in a collection of stories, is quite another matter.

[58] "Flight," *Pigeon Feathers,* p. 49.

work in a department store selling cheap fabrics at $14.00 a week, and how he, Allen Dow, made out with the girls when he was in high school particularly when at the age of seventeen he was chosen, along with three girls, to represent his high school in a debate at another high school a hundred miles away from Olinger, his hometown, and how he and Molly Bingaman, one of the girl debaters, got along ("her lipstick smeared in little unflattering flecks into the skin around her mouth; it was as if I had been given a face to eat"),[59] and how he finally breaks from his mother, severs the umbilicus, you might say, by having a series of almost consummated sexual encounters with Molly, after the last of which he "went to the all-night diner just beyond the Olinger town line and ate three hamburgers, ordering them one at a time, and drank two glasses of milk." [60]

With no attempt to belittle Updike, all I can say is that by this time it is of little concern to me whether Allen Dow ate three hamburgers that night, ordering them one at a time, and drank two glasses of milk, or ate two hamburgers and drank three glasses of milk, ordering *them* one at a time.

✳

Among many other American short story writers since 1940[61] who have concerned themselves primarily with contemporary manners and mores, Roger Angell in *The Stone Arbor* (1960) has produced a virtual gallery of fictional types associated with the fiction of *The New Yorker,* where the author works and where all these stories were originally

[59] *Ibid.,* p. 63.
[60] *Ibid.,* p. 71.
[61] The large number of recent writers of manners forces me to comment on only a few whom I consider either representative, outstanding, or both.

published between 1946 and 1960. They include a well-paid and harried businessman—"I am selfish and tired, and vicariousness is what I crave";[62] a handsome divorcée who works on fashion accounts for a big advertising agency—"thin, rather tall, with good legs and a straight back";[63] a perceptive broker who had been a public relations officer during the war; a highly paid television executive. Except for their names, they would immediately find a place for themselves in most John Cheever stories. Like so many Cheeverites, they work within a boomerang's throw of Madison Avenue; they dress well, eat well, talk well, travel well, and do almost everything well—except live well and sleep well. They are frightened or bored, nostalgic or sad. Almost everything worries them—though theirs is a well-mannered, stiff-upper-lip worry—whether it be fear of nuclear destruction or concern with how best to take advantage of the low tariff on French wines. Within this framework of essentially stereotyped characters, situations, and attitudes, Angell is an expert performer. He is intelligent, perceptive, and urbane, and he writes intelligent, perceptive, and urbane stories. His fiction is as well-tailored as are most of his white-collar or mink-stole characters whose lives, narrated with skill and grace, dribble off into studiously unresolved endings which are usually as quiet and subdued as the civilized monotony of their participants' lives.[64]

[62] Roger Angell, "Castaways," *The Stone Arbor and Other Stories* (Boston: Little, Brown, 1960), p. 2.
[63] "Côte d'Azur," p. 219.
[64] Exceptions are "In an Early Winter," a chilling portrayal of marriage, and the title story in which the central character destroys the statue of a naked Roman goddess which adorns the stone arbor he had built for his wife years ago. Threatened by the destructive ugliness of contemporary life in the form of bulldozers which befoul his much-loved home place in an "obscene ritual" of progress, Jason Lowery's

Warren Beck's four collections of short stories[65] are intelligent and thoroughly adult. Though Beck's work is varied in
method and tone, among his favorite subjects is that of the
moral responsibility of adults in a world which is more often
than not unreasonable and unfathomable. "Detour in the
Dark," from what seems to me his best collection, *The Far
Whistle* (1951), is characteristic. An understanding father
and his young son are forced to spend the night in a dilapi-
dated, decrepit town. Throughout the long hours of tension,
the father tries to shield the son from the corruption and
moral decay that have destroyed the heart of the community.
In the morning, they are able to leave, and the experiences of
the night seem to the child like the vague memory of a bad
dream. The father, however, is sure that the victory is a
temporary one. Life, he believes, is a process of attrition
and loss, and a child's innocence will eventually be eroded
by shame and despair. Meanwhile, the father concludes, he
will preserve for the child, as long as he is able to, as much
security and safety as possible. Child and adult, the author
suggests, are alike the expendable hostages of a dark and un-
settled era, an idea restated in many of these carefully
wrought stories.

The stories of Harold Brodkey, *First Love and Other Sorrows* (1958), range from the St. Louis boyhood of a pleas-

---

outburst is one of the few positive acts Angell's characters seem capable of making.
[65] *The Blue Sash and Other Stories* (1941), *The First Fish and Other
Stories* (1947), *The Far Whistle and Other Stories* (1951), all published by the Antioch Press, Yellow Springs, Ohio. *The Rest is Silence
and Other Stories* (1963) was published by Alan Swallow, Denver.

ant, moderately sensitive protagonist to the early adulthood of the same, or similar, young man, including an undergraduate love affair at Harvard, marriage to an attractive Wellesley girl who as Laurie or Laura is the focal character of several stories, and a somewhat grumpy parenthood.[66] Brodkey's warmhearted concern with basic human relationships is in pleasant contrast to the "how god-awful things are" lamentations of some of his older contemporaries. Though his stories occasionally teeter on the edge of triviality, and though Laura for all her charm might have become a bore had the author devoted many more stories to her trials and tribulations, Brodkey rather miraculously avoids either sentimentality or self-consciousness. The surface simplicity of his stories is disarming; in prose which is as unassuming and unaffected as a series of entries in a journal he has effectively held up the mirror to his own segment of experience. Like Salinger and Updike, he sees the problems of youth clearly and depicts them with admirable awareness and skill.

Elizabeth Enright's (1909–) most successful stories similarly grow out of ordinary situations involving intelligent individuals; almost without exception her best work is that in which the drama exists in the minds and hearts of her characters and does not depend for effect upon unusual circumstances, tricks, or artifice.[67] The title story of her best collec-

[66] Brodkey's young men are, like Updike's, easily upset—by the children's crying, by a front door's sticking one time and opening freely at another, by a wife's purchase of an unneeded ashtray, and the like. See, for example, "The Dark Woman of the Sonnets," *First Love and Other Sorrows* (New York: Dial, 1958). Some of my comments originally appeared in my "Short Fiction vs. Long," *Saturday Review* (Jan. 25, 1958), p. 18.

[67] As she does in "One for the Collection" or "An Old-Fashioned Setting," both in *The Moment Before the Rain* (New York: Harcourt,

tion, *The Moment Before the Rain* (1955), for example, merely re-creates a few moments in the lives of an elderly man napping on a veranda and an elderly lady who watches him, yet during this brief interval the woman relives the high points of her life and the reader shares them with her—the early married years, her children and the "shrill twilight voices of the past," her love affair that caution maimed and time killed, her acceptance of the belief that time takes away everything eventually, including love, and her realization that no matter what she did with her life, things would have ended the same way anyway, with "an old man napping and an old woman watching him." [68]

Miss Enright is similarly successful in capturing the essence of childhood, from her depiction of the fearful dream world of a child whose parents have been killed in an accident to her fine story of a wandering day in the life of a neglected child, "The Playground." Among other things, the child watches a couple making love and rescues her companion from drowning; when she returns home at dusk, her reply to her mother's "What happened today?" is a laconic "'Swam. Played. Nothing much.'" [69]

Brace, 1955). Similarly, Miss Enright is less effective when she turns to an eccentric rustic like the beer-swigging Mrs. Schultz of "The House on the River," in *The Riddle of the Fly* (New York: Harcourt, Brace, 1959).

[68] *The Moment Before the Rain,* p. 61

[69] "The Playground," *The Moment Before the Rain,* p. 54. All three of Miss Enright's collections contain some good stories about children; it comes as no surprise to know that Miss Enright began her career as a writer and illustrator of children's books, one of which won a Newbery Award in 1939. Some of my comments on Miss Enright originally appeared in my "Mirror to Nature," *Saturday Review* (March 5, 1955), pp. 18–19.

Even the least consequential of Nancy Hale's (1908–) many short stories[70] are consistently entertaining; intelligent, highly civilized, and gracious even when she is letting her victim's blood, Miss Hale is an urbane and witty commentator on the changing American social scene. Her characters fight no battles to reform society or change the world. Their problems are essentially personal—how to live with or without their current spouses, how to dull the edge of inner hunger, how to adjust to a society indifferent to older standards of conduct or too hurried to allow time for contemplation and civilized personal relations. She creates with gentle malice the antagonism between a faded Virginia matriarch and her Yankee daughter-in-law in "The Pattern of Perfection," dissects a neurotic but likeable coed and her unresponsive teacher in "The Secret Garden," and in "The Fox" presents a serio-comic commentary on life among the Piedmont hunt-club gentry, highlighted by the character of a heavy-drinking, hard-riding, slow-thinking native son who reads only Gibbon and is convinced that intellectuality and morbidity are synonymous.[71]

Miss Hale is equally skillful in her narrative sketches and semi-autobiographical vignettes and reminiscences. Around such simple situations as a child's first day at school, a mother's reading to an ill child, or a visit to a university commencement, she can create meaningful and moving characters and moods. That she can perform these feats of legerdemain is as much a tribute to her sensitive appraisal of people and

---

[70] Miss Hale's collections include *The Earliest Dreams* (1936), *Between the Dark and the Daylight* (1943), *The Empress's Ring* (1955), and *The Pattern of Perfection* (1960), the first three published by Scribner, the last by Little, Brown. Some of my comments on Miss Hale originally appeared in my "Melancholy Among the Well-Heeled," *Saturday Review* (Sept. 10, 1955), p. 62.

[71] "The Secret Garden" and "The Fox" are in *The Empress's Ring*.

places as it is to her thoroughly disciplined and flexible control of her medium.

Edward Newhouse's (1911–) most important collection of short stories is *Many Are Called* (1951).[72] All of the adjectives used to praise the fiction of such *New Yorker* authors as Roger Angell, Robert M. Coates, John Cheever, and John Updike automatically come to mind when one first reads Newhouse. His stories are timely, effective, entertaining, resourceful, well disciplined, witty, and urbane. *Many Are Called* contains forty-two stories originally published between 1939 and 1950, all but three of them in *The New Yorker* where the Hungarian-born author has been a staff member most of his adult life. There is hardly a poor story among them. Like so many of his *New Yorker* associates Newhouse is a man of indisputable talent and a fine reporter with a good eye and ear. His stories effectively reconstruct the temper and mood of the war decade. They display a blotting-paper kind of ability to capture the essence of the jargon of the moment, whether it be the conversation of a group of combat Air Force personnel or the habitués of Jake's Third Avenue saloon. They reflect with similar accuracy the mood of the period. Newhouse's people think "correctly" and feel "right" about things, from the war, the uneasy peace, and flag-waving Babbitts who never saw a battlefield to the lethal potentiality of modern automobiles. In spite of the author's marked ability, however, his stories are characterized by a kind of bland competence. Although they are frequently effective when read singly, collectively

---

[72] Newhouse's other collections are *Anything Can Happen* (1941), and *The Iron Chain* (1946), both published by Harcourt, Brace. One from the first of these and two from the second are included in *Many Are Called* (New York: Sloane, 1951).

they tend to resemble a lovingly laundered madras jacket, the muted colors of which merge together in studied uniformity. The same thing can be said for his characters. For all their intelligence and goodwill, it is hard to remember one from another; like the well-tailored, attaché-case-carrying commuters striding importantly from train to taxi in the Grand Central Station, they disappear in a blurred, indecipherable mass. Somewhere along the line, apparently, Newhouse decided to take the cash and let the credit go; with the decision went the diminishing of a real talent.

Almost without exception, the best stories of J. F. Powers (1917–) are concerned with pastors, curates, and parishioners of the Catholic Church; never a seminarian, to the best of my knowledge, he writes of this world with remarkable familiarity and wry understanding. His stories are highly individualistic and highly disciplined; they illustrate the triumph of skill and insight over such unspectacular materials as Father Udovic's reaction to a strange letter which turns up in the collection plate, Father Fabre's efforts to obtain a table for his room, or a curate's dislike for his superior's cats.

Powers is so accomplished that the reader is likely to be unimpressed by his admirable control of all the elements in each of his stories, by his happy integration of incident and setting, characters and idea. Perhaps the main source of his success is a thoroughly adult vision which enables him to create characters who are good without approaching perfection, who possess or are capable of evil without *being* evil, who are laughable without becoming ridiculous, or foolish without needing to be institutionalized. Perhaps it is his remarkable sense of selectivity, his ability to isolate the significant from that which is merely interesting; his ability to select the inevitably right word, thought, detail, gesture, or incident. Perhaps it is his ability to suggest constantly the universal in the specific without recourse to the didactic or the ponderously symbolic.

Whatever the sources of his strength, Powers has succeeded in creating his corner of the universe, with its dedicated individuals and its crass opportunists, its winners and losers. Beneath the good humor and tolerance which characterize his treatment of characters, he presents brief but chilling glimpses into a way of life in which the trivial becomes confused with the momentous, in which the desire to serve mankind can result in service of self or in envy, greed, and occasional cruelty. He has created, in short, a special segment of the world which is very similar to the world outside the monastic walls.[73]

J. D. Salinger's (1919–) best short stories, as it seems to me they are in his relatively early collection, *Nine Stories* (1953), almost warrant the extravagant praise bestowed upon them by the hordes of sometimes frenzied Salingerphiles.[74] "A

---

[73] Characteristic is a detail such as Father Philbert's holding a crucifix over Father Malt's cat and then beating the animal ("Death of a Favorite," *The Presence of Grace* [New York: Doubleday, 1956], p. 42). The same kind of juxtaposition of opposites is frequently seen in Powers's first collection, *Prince of Darkness* (New York: Doubleday, 1947), and in his National Book Award–winning novel, *Morte d'Urban* (New York: Doubleday, 1962), several chapters of which were originally published as short stories. Some of my comments on Powers originally appeared in "The Tightrope Writers," *Virginia Quarterly Review* (Summer 1956), pp. 470–72.

[74] The first full-length study of Salinger's fiction is F. L. Gwynn and J. L. Blotner's *The Fiction of J. D. Salinger* (Pittsburg: Univ. of Pittsburg Press, 1958); the most recent is Warren French's *Salinger* (New York: Twayne, 1963). Both are good. In between there has been a deluge of articles, chapters of books, workbooks, explications, and the

Perfect Day for Bananafish," "Uncle Wiggily in Connecticut," "For Esmé—with Love and Squalor," and "The Laughing Man" are alive with a profound sensitivity to the significance of the nuances of the human experience. They are perceptive and warm, witty and wise. They move swiftly, and Salinger's dialogue is often a wonder to behold, as has been frequently observed. Above all, they pass the ultimate test of memorableness. Once having been read, they tend to become part of one's vicarious experience. They linger in the mind, disturbingly or pleasantly. They suggest more than they actually tell or depict and are animated by what Robert Penn Warren has called the "shadowy, unsaid, unreconciled meanings that . . . haunt every story worth writing or reading." [75]

Salinger's fiction, for all its freshness and originality, is frequently threatened by a curious kind of shadowy, lurking tendency toward cuteness. In his best stories this is somewhat like the slip of a well-groomed woman; one is vaguely aware that it probably exists, but it doesn't show. In what seems to me the unnecessarily elliptical "Pretty Face and Green My Eyes," or in the portrayal of Selena Graff and her leg-scratching brother and his apparently homosexual friend of "Just Before the War with the Eskimos," or in some of the passages in *Franny and Zooey* (1961) and *Raise High the Roof Beam, Carpenters* (1963), the slip becomes painfully or embarrassingly visible. One wishes that Salinger's people were not quite so enchanted with themselves or quite so self-congratulatory. Very voluble, very sensitive, very articu-

---

like, of uneven quality. Salinger has suffered more at the hands of his sometimes almost hysterical admirers than from his detractors.
[75] Robert Penn Warren, Introduction, Peter Taylor, *A Long Fourth and Other Stories* (New York: Harcourt, Brace, 1948), p. ix.

late, one sometimes feels that they would be more attractive
and sympathetic if they did not make it quite so clear that
like Cabell's Jurgen they considered themselves so mon-
strously clever.[76]

Although most of Irwin Shaw's (1913–) best-known short
stories concern war, racial intolerance, and similar "big" subjects and themes,[77] many of his stories of contemporary manners are extremely effective and have been frequently
praised and anthologized. Probably the best of these is "The
Eighty-Yard Run," with its memorable depiction of a disillusioned grade-B ex-athlete and the breakdown of his marriage to a pseudo-intellectual with grade-A aspirations. Other
good stories in this category include "The Girls in Their Summer Dresses," a deftly drawn vignette of a husband with a
roving eye, "The Climate of Insomnia," a searching characterization of a college professor who suspects wrongdoing in
almost everyone, "Main Currents of American Thought,"
"Search Through the Streets of the City," "Weep in Years to
Come," and "Widow's Meeting." [78]

[76] *Franny and Zooey* (Boston: Little, Brown, 1961) and *Raise High
the Roof Beam, Carpenters and Seymour—an Introduction* (Little,
Brown, 1963) for all their awareness, erudition, and wit seem to me
to be decidedly inferior to Salinger's earlier stories. Long-winded and
self-imitative, they sometimes justify Salinger's fears that his saga of
the New York Glasses might "sooner or later . . . bog down, perhaps
disappear entirely, in my own methods, locutions, and mannerisms"
(*Franny and Zooey*, dust jacket).
[77] Shaw's war and racial injustice stories are commented on in Chapter Six.
[78] All of the stories mentioned are in *Mixed Company; Collected
Stories of Irwin Shaw* (New York: Random House, 1950). In addition
to seven previously uncollected stories and one hitherto unpublished,
Mixed Company contains the best from Shaw's three previous volumes

Shaw's work is often over-contrived, over-simplified, and sentimentalized,[79] but it possesses the very great asset of seldom if ever being dull. He is a good storyteller who has created many a scene of cliff-hanging suspense, excitement, and high drama. He has created what is probably the most crowded gallery of vivid and diverse characters in recent short fiction, characters ranging from a statuesque belly dancer whose career is ruined when a middle-aged man puts an olive in her navel to men in gray flannel suits, loving apartment-dwellers, homesick Indians, and *weltschmerzig* continuity writers for the comic strips. He handles setting and place effectively, often expertly, whether they be a rundown New York hotel, a private tennis court, or a sidestreet in Paris. Whatever his shortcomings, he is probably the most versatile contemporary American short story writer around; for sheer versatility and variety, he can more profitably be compared with English writers like H. E. Bates or William Sansom than with his American colleagues.

Many other American short story writers have contributed to the revival of the story of manners. Some of these, like James Thurber, have already been recognized as writers of contemporary classics. Others, including Mary McCarthy, are better known as novelists even though they may not have done their best work in the longer form. Still others have been for the most part ignored. Of all fictional types, the story of manners is the form with which the average reader

---

of short stories, *Sailor Off the Bremen* (1939), *Welcome to the City* (1942), and *Act of Faith* (1946), all published by Random House. [79] Shaw's shortcomings are particularly apparent in his most recent collection, *Tip on a Dead Jockey* (New York: Random House, 1957). Only Shaw's extreme virtuosity and journalistic expertise remove most of these stories from the realm of competent slick fiction.

can most readily identify. It has, as we have seen, its generic weaknesses; it can easily lapse into preoccupation with the trivial, or it can become mannered, repetitious, self-imitative, or effete. Beneath its customary subdued mood and restrained manner, however, the story of manners at its best is concerned with the recurring truths of the human heart and with the day to day changes of contemporary society. It is capable of reminding the reader of the drama in the lives of average or non-exceptional people. It can reveal the extraordinary which is always present in the ordinary, of the universal which exists in the specific. Out of unspectacular events in the lives of "ordinary" human beings, the writer of manners suggests universal truths, creates universal images, and ponders universal enigmas.[80]

[80] Other notable collections of stories of manners, or volumes containing some notable stories of manners, include Louis Auchincloss's *The Injustice Collectors* (1950), *The Romantic Egoists* (1954), and *Powers of Attorney* (1963); Ludwig Bemelmans' *I Love You, I Love You, I Love You* (1942) and *Hotel Bemelmans* (1946); Sally Benson's *Women and Children First* (1946); Burton Bernstein's *The Grove* (1961); Kay Boyle's *Thirty Stories* (1946); Frank Brookhouser's *She Made the Big Town* (1952); Robert M. Coates's *All the Year Round* (1943) and *The Hour after Westerly* (1957); Evan S. Connell's *The Anatomy Lesson* (1957); Daniel Curley's *That Marriage Bed of Procrustes* (1957); George P. Elliott's *Among the Dangs* (1961); James T. Farrell's several collections, including *French Girls Are Vicious* (1955) and *A Dangerous Woman* (1957); Mavis Gallant's *The Other Paris* (1956); George Garrett's *King of the Mountain* (1957), *In the Briar Patch* (1961), and *Cold Ground Was My Bed Last Night* (1964); Martha Gellhorn's *Two by Two* (1958); Herbert Gold's *Love and Like* (1960); William Humphrey's *The Last Husband* (1953); Charles Jackson's *The Sunnier Side* (1950) and *Earthly Creatures* (1953); Christopher La Farge's *All Sorts and Kinds* (1949); Oliver La Farge's *A Pause in the Desert* (1957); Victoria Lincoln's *Grandmother and the Comet* (1944) and *Desert Water* (1963); Robert Lowry's *New*

York Call Girl (1958) and *Party of Dreamers* (1963); Robie Macauley's *The End of Pity* (1957); Mary McCarthy's *The Company She Keeps* (1942) and *Cast a Cold Eye* (1950); John McNulty's *The World of John McNulty* (1957); Joseph Mitchell's *McSorley's Wonderful Saloon* (1943); Tillie Olsen's *Tell Me a Riddle* (1961); Grace Paley's *The Little Disturbances of Man* (1959); Frances Gray Patton's *The Finer Things of Life* (1951); Dawn Powell's *Sunday, Monday, and Always* (1952); Philip Roth's *Goodbye, Columbus* (1959); William Saroyan's several collections, including *Dear Baby* (1945), *The Assyrian* (1950), and *The Whole Voyald* (1956); Mark Schorer's *The State of Mind* (1947); Budd Schulberg's *Some Faces in the Crowd* (1953); Delmore Schwartz's *The World Is a Wedding* (1948) and *Successful Love* (1961); Allan Seager's *The Old Man of the Mountain* (1950); Wallace Stegner's *The Women on the Wall* (1949) and *The City of the Living* (1956); Harvey Swados's *Nights in the Gardens of Brooklyn* (1960); James Thurber's *The Thurber Carnival* (1945); Mark Van Doren's *Collected Stories* (1962); Jerome Weidman's *My Father Sits in the Dark* (1961); Thomas Williams's *A High New House* (1963); Edmund Wilson's *Memoirs of Hecate County* (1946); Anne Goodwin Winslow's *Winter in Geneva and Other Stories* (1945); Richard Yates's *Eleven Kinds of Loneliness* (1962); Samuel Yellen's *The Passionate Shepherd* (1957).

I have discussed some of these authors in various other sections of this study; several additional authors discussed there might also be included here. I regret that the number and variety of good recent short story writers force me to indulge in the arbitrary and dubious luxury of "putting authors in categories," and I am aware that such classifying and categorizing has its disadvantages and occasional absurdities. The very first author on this list, Louis Auchincloss, is a case in point. For reasons which seem to me valid I have commented on this fine novelist and short story writer in the following chapter although his stories, whether they take place in a fashionable Long Island summer place or in the offices of a Wall Street law firm, are significant additions to the recent short fiction of manners.

5. "Sick in Mind and Body Both"

ENTAL and physical illness or abnormality have fasci-nated the creative imagination since the beginnings of written literature, but it was not until the middle decades of the twentieth century that the explosion occurred in the fictional depiction of the borderland between the "normal" and the "abnormal," between "sanity" and "madness," be-tween the "customary" and the "exceptional." During the forties and fifties, as understanding and treatment of mental illness moved slowly and painfully out of the dungeons cre-ated by ignorance, fear, and superstition, more and more fic-tion writers depicted the twilit half-world of the mentally ill with understanding and compassion.[1] Emotional violence, the desolation of the human spirit, madness, man's capacity for self-destruction, loneliness, withdrawal, separation, isolation, Oedipal fears, atavistic tyrannies, and all their attendant ills supplied subject matter and theme for more and more fiction writers. The depiction of the mentally ill and the emotionally maimed became one of the major directions taken by the American short story since 1940.[2]

[1] Prose fiction, long and short, became increasingly introspective during the last hundred years, more subjective than external, more concerned with exploring inner causes than with chronicling the external results of these causes. Historically, this tendency is seen with the Brontës in such "early" novels as *Jane Eyre* or *Wuthering Heights* or, with Dickens, in *The Mystery of Edwin Drood*, but the turning point in the history of English prose fiction occurred approximately half a century later in the writings of Conrad, James, and Joyce.

[2] Inevitably the customary camp followers and literary hyenas appeared on the scene to exploit what for decades had been a taboo of commercial fiction; by the end of the fifties much of the fiction of mental illness became as vulgar as a Neiman-Marcus Christmas catalogue. The couch of the psychiatrist threatened to replace the six-shooter of the Western lawman as stock property of fiction, motion picture, television, and cartoons. A contemporary mythology came into being, complete with its hierarchy of good guys versus bad guys (the kindly or the paranoid psychiatrist, the sadistic nurse or her compassionate counterpart, the patient who is less disturbed than his analyst). Of the many good books on the literary manifestations and applications of Freudian and post-Freudian psychology the following are particularly valuable: Frederick J. Hoffman, *Freudianism and the Literary Mind* (2nd ed.; Baton Rouge: Lousiana State Univ. Press, 1957); Simon O. Lesser, *Fiction and the Unconscious* (Boston: Beacon Press, 1957); Louis B. Fraiberg, *Psychoanalysis and American Literary Criticism* (Detroit: Wayne State Univ. Press, 1960), and Daniel E. Schneider, *The Psychoanalyst and the Artist* (New York: Farrar, Straus, 1950).

The World of Psychology, ed. G. B. Levitas (New York: Braziller, 1963), documents psychological theory and study with short stories or excerpts from novels and other literary forms which illustrate theses or theories of scientists, psychologists, and specialists in human behavior.

A similar preoccupation with the grotesque, the abnormal, and the bizarre is one of the major concerns of the recent American short story. Individuals like Jean Stafford's horrifyingly fat girl, Tennessee Williams's gigantic and cannibalistic black masseur, Flannery O'Connor's wooden-legged country girl, and Carson McCullers's malignant humpbacked dwarf people many of the most memorable stories of the past two decades. The grotesque—what in recent years has with increasing frequency been labeled American Gothic—has been an important element in prose fiction almost from its beginnings; the line of descent from "Monk" Lewis to Charles Dickens to William Faulkner is more direct than some of our early literary historians have indicated. Like Dickens and Faulkner, the best "New Gothic" writers tend to employ physical abnormality, exaggeration, and caricature to suggest the inner nature of a character or to indicate the essence of an individual who embodies universal traits and qualities. Beneath their eccentricities and abnormalities, the people of such diverse authors as James Purdy and Louis Auchincloss, Jean Stafford and Sylvia Berkman, Tennessee Williams and Charles Criswell are archetypes rather than mere freaks or biological mistakes, and as such are suggestive of the disorder of our times, not mere painted waxwork additions to Everybody's Chamber of Horrors.[3]

[3] Wolfgang Kayser, in *The Grotesque in Art and Literature* (trans. Ulrich Weisstein [Bloomington: Univ. of Indiana Press, 1963]), sees the sixteenth century, the pre-Romantic years, and our present era as periods in which the grotesque—"THE GROTESQUE IS THE ESTRANGED WORLD" (p. 184)—has been particularly dominant. The grotesque, he concludes, is the artistic expression of the alienation which grips mankind when belief in a perfect or protective natural order is weakened or destroyed.

Irving Malin defines the new Gothicism as the belief that the individual psyche is more important than society, that the disorder of the

Among the most distinguished recent American short stories concerned with mental or emotional disturbance and
the grotesque or the abnormal are those by James Purdy
(1923–), a native of Ohio, whose publishing history suggests
the difficulties encountered by an entire generation of individualistic, talented, offbeat American authors. For years

---

buried life must be charted, and that the typical New Gothic hero is a
weakling in a world depicted "decidedly out of focus." He discusses
this in connection with the fiction of Truman Capote, James Purdy,
Flannery O'Connor, John Hawkes, Carson McCullers, and J. D. Salinger in terms of narcissism or self-love, the family as an essentially destructive element, and in the use of such recurring symbols as the
haunted castle, the dark journey, and the reflection. (*New American
Gothic* [Carbondale: Southern Illinois Univ. Press, 1962].)

Ihab Hassan suggests that the contemporary self, discovering absurdity in the world, recoils "from the world, against itself"; the result
has been the development of a new protagonist in American fiction, the
anti-hero. The anti-hero, as Hassan sees him, has an almost saintly
capacity for pain and a criminal passion for heresy. Turning from
the disorder around him only to find chaos within, he cries out for
meaning, seeking it through love and religion. He remains, however,
shackled in self, and either fails to find any meaning in life, or achieves
only fragmentary or limited understanding. (*Radical Innocence: Studies in the Contemporary American Novel* [Princeton: Princeton Univ.
Press, 1961].)

In "The Grotesque: an American Genre," William Van O'Connor
comments on the American fiction writer's preoccupation with the "ir-
rational, the unpredictable, the bizarre, [and] . . . the grotesque,"
summarizes what previous writers from Hugo to Mann have had to say
about the grotesque, and concludes that "modern literature has sought
to incorporate the antipoetic into the traditionally poetic, the cowardly
into the heroic, the ignoble into the noble, the realistic into the romantic, the ugly into the beautiful. . . ." (*The Grotesque; An American
Genre and Other Essays* [Carbondale: Southern Illinois Univ. Press,
1962], pp. 4, 19.)

Sherwood Anderson's "grotesques" are for the most part "average,"

Purdy's stories were rejected by editor after editor until a few eventually found their way into such relatively obscure "little" magazines as *Prairie Schooner* and the *Black Mountain Review*. Eventually, in 1956, a group of Chicago businessmen subsidized and privately distributed his collection of nine strange and haunting stories, *Don't Call Me by My Right Name*. In the same year his novella, *63: Dream Palace*, now regarded as a contemporary classic by such dissimilar critics as David Daiches, Dame Edith Sitwell, and Dorothy Parker, was similarly financed and published. In expurgated form these two volumes were published in London in 1957 and won enthusiastic praise from several British critics. Only after this success was the book published in America as *Color of Darkness*, also in 1957;[4] like its English predecessor, the volume was an outstanding critical success, if not a financial

---

non-exceptional people (an immediate exception, of course, is Wing Biddlebaum of "Hands"). By the term "grotesques" Anderson is referring primarily to an inner flaw or emotional weakness rather than external freakishness or clinical "unusualness" as such. "It was the truths," he says, "that made . . . people grotesques . . . the moment one of the people took one of the truths to himself, called it his truth, and tried to live his life by it, he became a grotesque and the truth he embraced became a falsehood." ("The Book of the Grotesque," *Winesburg, Ohio* [New York: Modern Library, n.d.] p. 5.)

[4] Surprisingly, it was apparently Malcolm Cowley who first prevented Purdy from being published commercially in America. Mr. Cowley objected to *63: Dream Palace* on the grounds that it was "obscene and poorly-written" and objected even more strongly to *Malcolm* when he read it in manuscript. Victor Gollancz, the publisher of the first English edition, excluded many words from the original text, and also eliminated the title story, "Color of Darkness," and "You May Safely Gaze," and subsequently refused to publish *Malcolm* "on the grounds that it was unintelligible." (Letters from James Purdy to Peden, April 6, 1963, and April 20, 1963.)

one, as were Purdy's two novels, *Malcolm* (1959) and *The Nephew* (1960), and his most recent collection of eleven short stories and two plays, *Children Is All* (1962).

With only occasional examples the characters of *Color of Darkness* and *Children Is All* are either emotional or physiological misfits or both. Lonely, lost, isolated, unloved, or undesirable, they are confined within private hells which are sometimes of their own making and sometimes created by forces over which they can exercise little if any control. In the controversial *63: Dream Palace*, nineteen-year-old Fenton Riddleway and his younger, half-demented brother Claire, are living in a moldering rattrap of a decaying house on Manhattan's 63rd Street. Fenton becomes involved with a neurotic novelist and an assorted group of homosexuals, derelicts, and oddballs, including the alcoholic and ambiguous "great-woman." Claire, meanwhile, is dying. In his confused, amoral fashion, Fenton loves his brother and has tried to help him since the death of their mother. In his mind, love and hate are inextricably mingled—"just as he had wished Mama dead, so that he felt the agent of her death, so now he wanted Claire to be dead, and despite the fact that the only two people in the world he had loved were Mama and Claire." [5] If they were "safe from trouble," Fenton would be kind to Claire, but trouble is their destiny, and trouble always makes Fenton "mean." One night, after an almost intolerable scene involving a production of "Othello" by a group of homosexuals with whom Fenton has been associating, Fenton comes home drunk and murders Claire. He refuses to allow himself to accept the fact that his brother is dead, but after several harrowing days and nights he knows that Claire must have a "service, a funeral"; he must be put

[5] James Purdy, *Color of Darkness. Eleven Stories and a Novella* (Norfolk, Conn.: New Directions, 1957), p. 130.

in a "sheltered place." Fenton gets an old chest from the attic, not a "fragrant cedar chest" such as he had desired, but an "old white box with broken hinges and whose inside lid was covered with a filthy cloth." Finally—Cain having killed Abel, and out of love rather than hate[6]—he nerves himself for the task at hand:

> It took him all night to get himself ready to carry Claire up, as though once he had put him in the chest, he was really at last dead forever. For part of the night he found that he had fallen asleep over Claire's body, and at the very end before he carried him upstairs and deposited him, he forced himself to kiss the dead stained lips he had stopped and said, 'Up we go then, motherfucker.' [7]

Here, as in most of the *Color of Darkness* stories, Purdy has created a somber world of shocking paradox and violent contrasts in which love and hate are so closely related as to be indistinguishable, in which traditional personal or societal relationships are confused or altered almost beyond recognition.

Similarly, the sick child who is the central character of "Why Can't They Tell You Why?" moons over the picture of his father who had been killed during the war. His mother, an "ugly pale woman . . . [with] a faint smell from her like that of an uncovered cistern," threatens to send him to the "mental hospital with the bars . . . where they sent Aunt Grace." But the child cannot tear himself away from the pictures—"They're Daddy," he screams—until the mother, in a frenzy of rage and stupidity, attempts to force the boy to destroy them. Unsuccessful, the mother seizes some of the

[6] As Del Kolve has observed in "James Purdy: an Assessment," *Time and Tide* (March 23, 1961), p. 476.
[7] *63: Dream Palace*, p. 175.

pictures and hurls them into the fire. She turns to get the re-
mainder but, even in her thick-witted mind, she is appalled.
Her son no longer looks like a human child but "in his small
unmended night shirt like some crippled and dying animal
running hopelessly from its pain." She takes a step toward
him, but "the final sight of him made her stop. He had
crouched on the floor, and, bending his stomach over the
boxes, hissed at her, so that she stopped short, not seeing any
way to get at him, seeing no way to bring him back, while
from his mouth black thick strings of something slipped out,
as though he had spewed out the heart of his grief." [8]

Another lonely child, in the title story, is depicted as
slowly retreating into a limbo of hate and misunderstanding.
In a shocking scene the child viciously kicks and shouts ob-
scenities at his kindly but inadequate father who, at the
story's end, lies helpless and confused on the floor, writhing
with a physical agony less searing than the emotional shock
and damage occasioned by his son's attack. In "The Cutting
Edge," the artist son of unimaginative but reasonably well-
intentioned parents shaves his beard before returning to the
mother and father whom he finally "hates" and "despises"
for "what both of you have done to yourselves." [9] "Everything had come to the end" to the well-meaning man who is
fired from his job because he is suspected—rightly or wrongly
we are never told—of being a homosexual. [10] The wife of a
paraplegic, shut off from her war-casualty husband, is tempted
to strike him across the face when he is suffering most, and is
obsessed with the desire to buy a raven whose refrain is
George is dead. [11] A husband strikes his wife at a party because she hates his name; later, outside, he knocks her down

[8] "Why Can't They Tell You Why?" pp. 44, 47, 49.
[9] "Cutting Edge," p. 108.
[10] "Man and Wife."
[11] "Sound of Talking."

where she lies quite casually before erupting into terrible screams. " 'My God . . . I am in awful pain,' " she screams and the story ends flatly, as do so many of Purdy's stories, with her almost laconic statement, " 'Can't you see I'm bleeding?' " [12]

These and similar characters from *Color of Darkness* exist in a world dominated by sickness and despair. It is impossible to contemplate this world without a shudder of revulsion as well as pity; these are not stories for the squeamish or the rigidly orthodox. Yet Purdy is ruthlessly and unsparingly honest in creating his own segment of a world bereft of traditional values, and nowhere does he depict the morbid, the sensational, or the decadent for their own sakes alone.[13]

The stories in *Children Is All,* published five years after *Color of Darkness,* at first reading tend to lack the fierce and shocking impact of Purdy's earlier short fiction. "Everything Under the Sun" presents two lost and lonely youthful deviates reminiscent of Fenton and Claire Riddleway, and the prose poem "Sermon" takes the reader to the realm of a faceless, voiceless, and doomed audience. Such stories owe much of their effect to Purdy's effective use of the bizarre and the grotesque, as does the nightmarish short play, "Cracks," which is highlighted by another of the author's depictions of an unforgettable child. The world of the *Children Is All* stories, however, and the situations out of which most of the stories evolve, tend to be more immediately recognizable than those of *Color of Darkness.*

In "Home by Dark," for example, a grandfather and his grandson sit quietly at dusk, talking of the boy's dead parents

[12] "Don't Call Me by My Right Name," p. 31.
[13] Some of these comments appeared originally in my "And Never a Silver Lining," *New York Times Book Review* (Dec. 29, 1957), p. 4, and in "Short Fiction vs. Long," *Saturday Review* (Jan. 25, 1958), pp. 17–18.

and doing nothing more spectacular than to search for the child's tooth that has dropped into the grass. But as the twilight silently, deeply, descends, the exterior dark is paralleled and counterpointed by an inner illumination—paradoxically, an illumination of darkness—as a slow tide of grief overwhelms the old man who "pushes the boy's head tight against his breast so he would not hear the sounds that came out now like a confused and trackless torrent, making ridiculous the quiet of evening." [14]

The revelation of nameless fear or grief or revulsion is similarly unspectacular in such stories as "The Lesson," in which an aggressively masculine swimming instructor attracts and repels a teenage swimmer who finally cries out: " 'Go away, please. . . . Don't lean over me, please, and let the water fall from you on me. Please, please, go back into the pool. I don't want you close now. Go back into the pool.' " [15]

In the same subdued manner, one of the most effective of the *Children Is All* stories, "The Encore," is built around a quietly desperate scene involving the gulf between a well-meaning but uneducated mother and her unpopular intellectual son. "Mrs. Benson" is an equally quiet though less effective character delineation of a mother and daughter chatting in a Paris café. "Daddy Wolf," on the other hand, is more typically early Purdy. This is a wild, weird monologue of an unbalanced, semi-literate man who pours out his problems and fears to an Advice-to-the-Troubled commentator: he's afraid of rats, his wife has left him because she heard that the V.D. rate was going up. In less skilled hands, such a story might end in caricature or burlesque. As it is, how-

[14] "Home by Dark," *Children Is All* (Norfolk, Conn.: New Directions, 1962), p. 23.
[15] "The Lesson," p. 45.

ever, "Daddy Wolf" is an impressive tour de force, memorable both for its characterization and for its lyrically nightmarish quality. In somewhat similar fashion, "Goodnight,
Sweetheart" hovers upon the abyss of the ludicrous, but
avoids the abyss, and is a moving picture of terrible loneliness. An elderly schoolteacher somewhat reminiscent of
Sherwood Anderson's Kate Swift–Alice Hindman, Miss Mi-
randa walks naked to the home of the young bachelor she
had taught some years before, and finally persuades him to
join her in the bed. Nothing, of course, happens. They are,
in reality, miles and miles apart even while they "lay . . .
close to one another, and they both muttered to themselves
in the darkness as if they were separated by different
rooms. . . ." [16]

Loneliness, the inability to communicate, and the slow
withdrawal into the private hells of the unwanted appear
and reappear in both the *Color of Darkness* and the *Children
Is All* stories which are like stones suddenly glimpsed in
swiftly moving streams and transmuted into something
strange, wonderful, and unusual.

It is as a prose poet of the abnormal, the unbalanced, and
the grotesque that Purdy has achieved his highest successes.
There is nothing grotesque, however, about his narrative
method. Except for such long pieces as 63: *Dream Palace* or
the monologues of "Daddy Wolf" or "The Sermon," his
stories are almost classical in their simplicity, in their time
span (most of them occur within a few minutes or at the most
an hour or two of elapsed chronological time), in their simplicity of setting, and in their limited *dramatis personae.*
Purdy writes without pretentiousness, artiness, or exhibi-
tionism, and relies for the most part on the use of external
scene and a relaxed, almost laconic dialogue reminiscent of

[16] "Goodnight, Sweetheart," p. 108.

Hemingway and O'Hara without being in any way imitative. Quite the contrary, Purdy is as individualistic as a blue unicorn and at his best can do more with a whisper than most fiction writers do with a shout, as Dame Edith Sitwell has observed.[17]

Beneath the simple and relaxed exterior of his stories, beneath such disarmingly superficial devices as the talk about food in such a story as "About Jessie Mae," [18] the reader is allowed brief glimpses into a world in which the familiar suddenly becomes strange and terrible, as though one walking through a well-known terrain were to find himself without warning at the edge of a void alive with sights and sounds only partly recognizable. Purdy's is a strange, highly individual talent. His awareness of the murky depths of human cruelty or indifference is as startling as his recognition of their opposites. He is preoccupied with the recurring themes of loneliness and isolation, and with the paradoxes he sees inherent in the human situation—love-hate, beauty-ugliness, compassion-cruelty. Out of these paradoxes and in terms of these themes, Purdy is creating a fictional world uniquely his own.[19]

The smell of the sick room permeates the thoughtful, carefully wrought stories of Jean Stafford (1915–) collected in *Children Are Bored on Sunday* (1953), and *Stories: Jean Stafford, John Cheever, Daniel Fuchs, William Maxwell*

[17] Edith Sitwell, Preface, *Color of Darkness* (Philadelphia: Lippincott, 1961), p. 9.
[18] "About Jessie Mae" is in *Children Is All*.
[19] Some of these conclusions, as well as most of my comments about the *Children Is All* stories, originally appeared in my "Out of Contrasts Two Fictional Worlds," *Virginia Quarterly Review* (Spring 1963), pp. 345–47.

(1956). With very few exceptions physical maladies, individual peculiarities, or private misfortunes force her characters to withdraw from the world of customary urges and responses into a sick world of unfulfilled longings and desires.

"A Country Love Story" is characteristic. It is one of Miss Stafford's best stories and one of the most moving recent treatments of the breakup of a marriage and the withdrawal into the world of the mentally ill. May, an intelligent, sensitive young woman married to a historian twenty years older than she, moves to a "solemn hinterland" following Daniel's recovery from tuberculosis. Daniel retreats more and more into the world of his research until May gradually is aware that love, "the very center of their being, was choked off, overgrown, invisible." [20] As Daniel's indifference slowly deepens into hatred and cruelty, May creates an imaginary lover. Eventually she not only believes in this lover's existence, but depends "wholly on his companionship." In her mind she betrays Daniel constantly; her sin becomes frighteningly real to her, a longing and a need which allow her no peace. Finally, after Daniel has accused her openly of "going mad," she fancies that the lover is sitting in the old-fashioned sleigh in the front yard of their country home. After a hideous scene in which Daniel destroys the last of May's illusions, she has nowhere to go but to the sleigh, now empty except for a blacksmith's cat which has curled upon the seat. May now realizes that "no change would come, and that she would never see her lover again. Confounded utterly, like an orphan in solitary confinement, she went outdoors and got into the sleigh. The blacksmith's imperturbable cat stretched and rearranged his position, and May sat

[20] Jean Stafford, "A Country Love Story," *Children Are Bored on Sunday* (New York: Harcourt, Brace, 1953), p. 48. Unless otherwise noted, references are to this volume.

beside him with her hands locked tightly in her lap, rapidly
wondering over and over again how she would live the rest
of her life." [21]

May, alone, unloved, and lost, is characteristic of Miss
Stafford's people. Sickness, loneliness, the need to communicate but the inability to do so are common to all her stories.
Ramona, the hideously fat young woman of "The Echo and
the Nemesis," is hagridden by an enormous appetite. She
sees herself in dreams as "nothing but an enormous mouth
and a tongue, trembling lasciviously," and seeks escape in
fabricating the myth of a beautiful twin sister who died
young, but who is in reality her own lost beauty before eating
became a disease and a madness, a beauty "dead, dead and
buried under layers and layers of fat." [22]

Similarly, Pansy Vanneman, the young girl of "The Interior Castle," who has suffered terrible head and face injuries
in an automobile accident. Lying in a nightmare world of
pain and fear, Pansy retreats into a "world which she had
created." Confronted by relentless, unyielding pain which
advances upon her like an army with banners, Pansy contemplates her brain, "a jewel . . . a flower . . . always
pink and always fragile, always deeply interior and invalua-
ble." She begins to love not life or the hope of recovery, but
her own spirit, "enclosed within her head." She fears that
the doctor might maim it, "might leave a scratch on one of
the brilliant facets of the jewel, bruise a petal of the flower,
smudge the glass where the light burned, blot the envelopes,
and that then she would die or would go mad." [23]

Similar, too, are the charming Beatrice Trueblood of "Beatrice Trueblood's Story" who wills herself, as it were, into
deafness and is separated by this physical difference, which

[21] *Ibid.*, 60.
[22] "The Echo and the Nemesis," pp. 23, 36.
[23] "The Interior Castle," pp. 200, 203.

virtually amounts to a stigmata, from friendship, love, and
society; or the alcoholic young mother, reminiscing of her
youthful quest for education, and romance, who gazes upon
the gray landscape and confesses "I do not know whether it
is forever midnight or forever noon." [24]

Some of Miss Stafford's characters display their eccentricities proudly; others are unaware of their unusualness
which sets them apart from their fellows until it erupts in an
act of unpremeditated violence. Ramona of "The Echo and
the Nemesis" looks at the world through the wrong end of a
pair of binoculars. The refugee doctor of "The Home Front"
virtually has a love affair with a cat, his "dearest friend,"
nearly goes into "a tailspin" at the sight of a rose in the hair
of one of the boarders, and retches at the sight of a boy
burning caterpillars. A Bostonian living with his mother in
a rundown house wears a stock to cover a wen, smells of
Necco wafers, and walks through doors backwards.[25] A ship's
captain refuses to eat a roasted Negro infant and Mrs. Baum-
gartner, a "delicious blonde," is beaten by her husband with
a ski pole in the railroad station at Boise.[26]

Whether she writes in the grotesque, almost masquelike
manner of "A Modest Proposal" or with the straightforward
realism of "A Summer Day," Miss Stafford is a skilled and
disciplined artist who creates painstakingly in prose of admirable texture. She develops her characters slowly, often
with a leisureliness reminiscent of Henry James. Never does
she force her ideas upon the reader; there are few Q.E.D.'s
in her fiction. Rather, she presents her characters and situations with at times almost Kafkaesque ambiguity. Her world
is a limited one into which sunlight and fresh air seldom

[24] "A Winter's Tale," in *New Short Novels*, ed. Mary Louise Aswell
(New York: Ballantine Books, 1954), p. 145.
[25] "The Bleeding Heart."
[26] "A Modest Proposal."

penetrate; the odor of decay and death hovers over it.[27] Richly colored, varied, often grotesque in their contrasts, her stories are like Japanese water shells which open silently to disgorge a phantasmagoria of brightly colored paper flowers in marked contrast to the bland, unrevealing forms in which they are contained.[28]

The short stories of Tennessee Williams (1914–), collected in *One Arm* (1948) and *Hard Candy* (1954),[29] have been largely overshadowed by the author's continuing success and notoriety as a playwright. In addition to possessing special interest as occasionally being the first or early versions of characters and situations eventually developed into full-length plays,[30] Williams's stories are important in their

[27] An exception is "Maggie Meriwether's Rich Experience," in which Maggie, a Tennessee girl, is contrasted with a group of decaying aristocrats. An excellent characterization, Maggie is one of Miss Stafford's few "normal" or happy protagonists (from *Stories*).

[28] Some of these comments originally appeared in my "A Bleak, Sad World," *New York Times Book Review* (May 10, 1953), p. 5.

[29] *One Arm* was originally published in a limited edition in 1948, and in a trade edition in 1954 (*One Arm and Other Stories* [Norfolk, Conn.: New Directions]). *Hard Candy, A Book of Stories* was published in a limited edition in 1954, also by New Directions. The quotations from *One Arm* are from the trade edition.

[30] The relationships between the stories and the plays—between "Portrait of a Girl in Glass" and *The Glass Menagerie*, "The Yellow Bird" and *Summer and Smoke*, "Three Players of a Summer Game" and *Cat on a Hot Tin Roof*, and "Night of the Iguana" and the play of the same name—are commented on briefly by Benjamin Nelson in *Tennessee Williams. The Man and His Work* (New York: Obolensky, 1961), p. 185. They are not discussed in other recent critical biographies, Signi Lenea Falk's *Tennessee Williams* (New York: Twayne, 1961) or Nancy Tischler's *Tennessee Williams: Rebellious Puritan* (New York: Citadel Press, 1961). The Nelson biography contains a good discussion of Williams's short stories, pp. 185–97.

own right and are at their best a permanent addition to the "sick" fiction of the forties and fifties.

The world of Williams's stories possesses considerable variety of method, yet at the same time it is as limited and circumscribed as Poe's, which in some ways it resembles. His stories are alike in their preoccupation with what one Williams character speaks of as the "sense of the enormous grotesquerie of the world." [31] They are permeated, too, with an air of profound melancholy, and iridescent with a faded beauty and corruption which recalls John Randolph's irreverent simile of a rotting mackerel in the moonlight, that "shines and stinks, and stinks and shines." Similar character types appear and reappear throughout Williams's stories: disillusioned or frustrated artists and intellectuals, sex-starved virgins or nymphomaniacs, faded gentlewomen and hypocritical clergymen, homosexuals and alcoholics, destructive women and likeable adolescents. Recurring motifs include decay, disease, abnormality, and above all *loss,* loss through the inexorable process of time and the subsequent fall from grace, a fall more often physiological than spiritual.

With almost no exceptions, Williams's people are adrift, unloved, and unwanted. Heredity often plays an important part in their alienation from "normal" or "approved" standards of conduct; their deterioration is hastened or precipitated further by ironies of circumstance over which they have no control; they are exploited by their friends or family, or slowly and often passively strangled by their own weaknesses and fear. "To love is to lose," Williams once wrote,[32] and in one way or other his characters are losers, not winners.

[31] "The Night of the Iguana," *One Arm,* p. 188.
[32] In Williams's Foreword to *Sweet Bird of Youth* (Norfolk, Conn.: New Directions, 1959), p. viii.

To alter his statement to "To live is to lose" would suggest the common chord of his short fiction.

With few exceptions, Williams's best stories are those concerned with basically non-exceptional characters who are depicted with an understanding, sympathy, and compassion which makes ridiculous the comment that Williams, like Hardy, is a sadist who creates his people only to humiliate them. Perhaps the most memorable and the most moving of these stories is "Portrait of a Girl in Glass," with its depiction of the shy and introverted Laura, the "petals" of whose mind had simply closed with fear and who could make no "positive motion toward the world but stood at the edge of the water, so to speak, with feet that anticipated too much cold to move" [33] and who was to become the most appealing character in what still seems to be Williams's most moving play, *The Glass Menagerie.*

Characteristic, too, of this group of quiet, non-sensational stories is one of Williams's earliest, the first published under his own name, "The Field of Blue Children," an account of a transitory love affair between a young poet, Homer Stallcup, and an undergraduate sorority girl with minor literary aspirations. Homer, an "outsider," is encouraged by Myra, an "insider." They come together for a moment of love in a field of blue flowers, and subsequently drift apart. Myra marries an unexciting fraternity boy and slips into a humdrum marriage, and Homer simply fades out of her life.

Yet the memory of the incident in the field of blue flowers persists. Myra seldom feels "restless anymore" and abandons her verse writing; her "life seemed to be perfectly full without it." But she is impelled, one late spring evening several years after her marriage, to return to the scene of her first encounter with love.

[33] "Portrait of a Girl in Glass," *One Arm,* p. 97.

The field was exactly as she had remembered it. She walked quickly out among the flowers; then suddenly fell to her knees among them, sobbing. She cried for a long time . . . and then she rose to her feet and carefully brushed off her skirt and stockings. Now she felt perfectly calm and in possession of herself once more. She went back to the car. She knew that she would never do such a ridiculous thing as this again, for now she had left the last of her troublesome youth behind her.[34]

With its muted lyricism and its lowly diminishing cadences—"The whole field was covered with dancing blue flowers. There was a wind scudding through them and they broke before it in pale blue waves, sending up a soft whispering sound like the infinitely diminished crying of small children at play" [35]—the story reminds us that if Williams achieved fame as a playwright, he began his career as a dedicated and essentially traditional poet.

Equally memorable and depicted with similar understanding and compassion are the brother and sister of the presumably autobiographical story of adolescence and death, "The Resemblance Between a Violin Case and a Coffin," which is a moving study of the loss of innocence and youth and beauty. Almost as impressive are Williams's characterizations of the awkward college students in "The Important Thing," and the actor protagonist of "The Vine" who is finally forced to accept the fact that he is washed up. His confrontation with the truth—all defenses broken, all illusions stripped from him—is one of the high marks in Williams's fiction.[36]

[34] "The Field of Blue Children," *One Arm*, p. 166.
[35] *Ibid.*, p. 164.
[36] "The Resemblance Between a Violin Case and a Coffin" and "The Vine" are in *Hard Candy*; "The Important Thing" is in *One Arm*.

Perhaps the best of all of Williams's fictional creations is
Brick Pollitt of "Three Players of a Summer Game." Delta
planter, onetime famous Sewanee athlete, and dedicated
alcoholic, Brick is eventually emasculated, spiritually and
emotionally if not physically, by Margaret, one of the most
destructive of Williams's predatory contemporary vampires
("It was as though she had her lips fastened to some invisible wound in his body through which drained out of him
and flowed into her the assurance and vitality that he had
owned before marriage"). By the end of the story, Brick is a
pitiable ruin, driven through the streets in a Pierce Ar-
row by Margaret, "clothed and barbered with his usual im-
maculacy, so that he looked from some distance like the
president of a good social fraternity in a gentleman's college
of the South," but no longer a man, indeed no longer a human being, but a babbling and goggling wreck "sheepishly
grinning and nodding," while Margaret gaily blows the
"car's silver trumpet at every intersection," waving and call-
ing to everybody "as if she were running for office," while
Brick "nodded and grinned with senseless amiability behind
her. It was exactly the way that some ancient conqueror,
such as Caesar or Alexander the Great or Hannibal, might
have led in chains through a captive city the prince of a state
newly conquered."

Though he is unforgettably individualized, Brick Pollitt,
like so many of Williams's people, is an effectively function-
ing symbol, in this case of waste, the waste of human grace
and beauty and dignity. Such waste, and the attritions of
time, are twin villains in Williams's view of the world. "Physical beauty," the narrator of "Three Players of a Summer
Game," comments, is "of all human attributes the most in-
continently used and wasted, as if whoever made it despised it, since it is made so often only to be disgraced by

painful degrees and drawn through the streets in chains." [37]

These are Williams's great betrayers: waste and time together, they degrade and befoul, and are unconquerable.

A second group of Williams's short fiction tends to center around characters who are pathological or societal outcasts and rejects. Here again, Williams is concerned with the loss of beauty and grace, and with the attritions of time, along with an almost obsessive preoccupation with homosexuality, decay, and degradation. The best of these stories is "One Arm," set in the vicinity of New Orleans which Williams knew so well and utilizes so effectively. Oliver Winemiller, apparently no kin to Alma Winemiller of *Summer and Smoke,* had been lightheavyweight boxing champion of the Pacific Fleet but subsequently loses his arm in an automobile accident. His degeneration and deterioration are rapid: Oliver becomes a male hustler, a notorious homosexual, and finally murders a wealthy man who had paid him to act in a "blue" movie. In jail, awaiting execution, Oliver finally feels the passion and desire which he had for so many years aroused in others. But it is of course too late, and Oliver goes to the chair lost and broken, incomplete and unfulfilled, with "all his debts unpaid." Even in death, however, there is about Oliver something of the heroic, the beautiful. Unclaimed, Oliver's body becomes a cadaver in the medical school. The dissectors are "somewhat abashed by the body under their knives. It seemed intended for some more august purpose, to stand in a gallery of antique sculpture, touched only by light through stillness and contemplation, for it had the nobility of some broken Apollo that no one was likely to carve so purely again." [38]

There is similar pathos but very little similar nobility in

[37] "Three Players of a Summer Game," *Hard Candy,* pp. 14, 43, 44.
[38] "One Arm," *One Arm,* p. 29.

the unhappy lives of most of Williams's other deviates. One can feel sorry for Edith Jelkes, the sex-starved spinster of "The Night of the Iguana," whom we are introduced to in Acapulco where she is recuperating after having suffered "a sort of nervous breakdown" at the Mississippi Episcopal school where she had taught art. Like many of Williams's genteel no-longer-young ladies with a penchant for disaster, Edith is the victim of hereditary taints, and to that extent is only partially responsible for her actions.[39] Her dubious sexual triumph over a homosexual writer, however, is hardly cause for unlimited rejoicing. The writer himself, moreover, and his male companion, both of whom alternately attract and repel Edith, are essentially flat characters who fail to engage either our sympathy or dislike.

It is similarly difficult to sympathize with the two derelicts of "Two on a Party," one of the loneliest, saddest couples in recent literature. Billy is a onetime English instructor and Hollywood hackwriter who is currently a self-destroying egoist; Cora is a kindly lush with "none of that desire to manage and dominate which is a typically American perversion of the female nature." [40] Each of these whores is sympathetically observed and as convincing as a thunderstorm, and the terrible emptiness of their lives "on the road" is

[39] "She belonged to an historical Southern family of great but now moribund vitality whose latter generations had tended to split into two antithetical types, one in which the libido was pathologically distended and another in which it would seem to be all but dried up. The households were turbulently split and so, fairly often, were the personalities of their inmates. There had been an efflorescence among them of nervous talents and sickness, of drunkards and poets, gifted artists and sexual degenerates, together with fanatically proper and squeamish old ladies of both sexes who were condemned to live beneath the same roof with relatives whom they could only regard as monsters." ("The Night of the Iguana," *One Arm,* p. 170.)

[40] "Two on a Party," *Hard Candy,* p. 57.

chillingly portrayed. But in the final analysis their story is as empty as their lives; Billy's only concern, apparently, is his fall from physiological grace and his morbid horror of his premature baldness, and Cora tends to fade into the background as the story progresses. Like the cancer-ridden protagonist of "The Mysteries of the Joy Rio" who is compelled to return to the seedy theater where in the past he had enjoyed sexual delights with an elderly man,[41] Billy and Cora's destruction evokes little more than morbid horror.

Like "Two on a Party" and "The Mysteries of the Joy Rio," Williams's fantasies are memorable in their presentation of decay and disintegration, and are alive with that "Sense of the Awful" which Williams has called the "desperate black root of nearly all significant modern art." [42] For the most part, however, the fantasies seem the least successful of his short fiction; in them the depiction of what one Williams character calls the "mad pilgrimage of the flesh" [43] frequently approaches caricature or burlesque.

Probably the most successful and the best known of these symbolic excursions into the province of the grotesque, the Gothic, and the hallucinated is "Desire and the Black Masseur." From his childhood, Anthony Burns "had betrayed an instinct for being included in things that swallowed him up." Unloved, unlovable, and a passive leaf in the stream of life, Burns "loved to sit in the back rows of the movies where the darkness absorbed him gently . . . like a particle of food dissolving in a big hot mouth." One day he goes to a Turkish bath where he is administered to by a gigantic black masseur. He is attracted to the Negro and eventually "adores" the giant. In return the giant "loves" him, tortures him, and

[41] "The Mysteries of the Joy Rio" is in *Hard Candy.*
[42] Tennessee Williams, Preface, Carson McCullers, *Reflections in a Golden Eye,* cited by Hassan, p. 216.
[43] "The Malediction," *One Arm,* p. 55.

eventually devours him, flesh and splintered bones. As he
drops the bones, "left over from Burns' atonement," into a
lake, the black masseur thinks: "It is perfect . . . it is now
completed!" Perfection and atonement, the story tells us,
have gradually evolved out of the antitheses of love and
hate, torture and delight. Meanwhile, the Negro, like some
strange being above and beyond earthly passions, moves on
to another city where he waits in a "white-curtained place,
serenely conscious of fate bringing . . . another, to suffer
atonement as it had been suffered by Burns . . . Mean-
time, slowly, with barely a thought of so doing, the earth's
whole population twisted and writhed beneath the manipu-
lation of night's black fingers and the white ones of day with
skeletons splintered and flesh reduced to pulp, as out of this
unlikely problem, the answer, perfection, was slowly evolved
through torture." [44]

Without raising the question of the author's purpose, or lack
of it, "Desire and the Black Masseur" tends to fail because
Williams makes no effort to bridge the gap between the
specific framework of character, incident, time and place,
and the allegorical, symbolic, or mythic. Though powerful
in its Poelike totality of effect of horror and madness, the
story tends to fall apart as a self-contained piece of fiction.
It is not fiction which suggests the universal in terms of the
specific; it is undigested and indigestable allegory. Similarly
"The Poet," the protagonist of which distills a liquor which
makes the world change color, leads a life of benevolent
anarchy, and retreats into silence with an "incubus in his
bosom, whose fierce little purplish knot of a head was but-
ting against his ribs and whose limbs were kicking and
squirming with convulsions." [45] "Yellow Bird," a burlesque
written in a mocking, bantering tone fortunately absent

[44] "Desire and the Black Masseur," *One Arm,* pp. 83, 93, 94.
[45] "The Poet," *One Arm,* pp. 64–65.

from Williams's other stories, is similarly unsuccessful. It is difficult to find either amusement or edification in this story of the unmarried daughter of a Protestant minister, pushing thirty and mad for life and excitement, who begins by smoking in the attic and ends on "Monkey-Wrench Corner" of New Orleans's Vieux Carrée.

The humor in a story like "The Yellow Bird" is more often than not elephantine, the irony ponderous. The narrative method is similarly heavy-handed, involving such commentaries as "Now from this point on the story takes a strange turn that may be highly disagreeable to some readers, if any still hoped it was going to avoid the fantastic," [46] which to most contemporary readers are likely to be as objectionable as those of Trollope. In spite of their defects, however, Williams's "blasted allegories"—the phrase, of course, is Hawthorne's—are a searing indictment of the cruelty and injustice of the world as the author sees it. Even at their least successful they have about them the same curious pathos that characterizes Williams's fiction in general.[47] Whatever his form, method, or mood, the mad pilgrimage comes to the same dead end. Earth, sooner or later, "destroys her crooked child." [48]

[46] "The Yellow Bird," *One Arm*, p. 209.
[47] Some of these comments originally appeared in my "Broken Apollos and Blasted Dreams," *Saturday Review* (Jan. 5, 1955), pp. 11–12.
[48] The phrase is from an untitled poem by Williams included in Benjamin Nelson's *Tennessee Williams*, p. 197:

> I think the strange, the crazed, the queer
> will have their holiday this year,
> I think for just a little while
> there will be pity for the wild.
>
> I think in places known as gay
> in secret clubs and private bars,

The "sick" subject matter and themes which dominate the short stories of James Purdy, Jean Stafford, and Tennessee Williams similarly often preoccupied such nineteenth-century Americans as Poe, Hawthorne, and Bierce. More recent individual stories from Sherwood Anderson's "Adventure," Conrad Aiken's "Silent Snow, Secret Snow," and Wilbur Daniel Steele's "How Beautiful with Shoes," to Faulkner's "A Rose for Emily" and J. D. Salinger's "A Perfect Day for Bananafish" have become classics of the genre. The deluge of sick stories is essentially, however, a product of the last two decades. In addition to the authors to be commented on in the following pages,[49] such diverse established writers as Hortense Calisher,[50] John Cheever,[51]

---

the damned will serenade the damned
with frantic drums and wild guitars.

I think for some uncertain reason,
mercy will be shown this season
to the lovely and misfit,
to the brilliant and deformed—

I think they will be housed and warmed
And fed and comforted awhile
before, with such a tender smile,
the earth destroys her crooked child.

(Reprinted by permission of Ivan Obolensky, Inc., New York, New York.)

[49] As was the case in the preceding chapter, the large amount of recent short fiction concerned with mental or emotional illness and Gothic or grotesque materials forces me to comment on only a few authors whose work seems to me to be outstanding or indicative of significant trends or both.

[50] In such stories as "Heartburn," "In Greenwich There Are Many Gravelled Walks," and "Letitia, Emeritus," from *In the Absence of*

Roald Dahl,[52] James T. Farrell,[53] Leslie Fiedler,[54] Nancy Hale,[55] Shirley Jackson,[56] Howard Nemerov,[57] Lillian Ross,[58]

Angels (Boston: Little, Brown, 1951), and "The Scream on Fifty-Seventh Street," from *Tale for the Mirror: A Novella and Other Stories* (Boston: Little, Brown, 1962). The first of these concerns a man who is convinced that "a form of newt or toad" is lodged within his chest, the second presents a group of alcoholics and homosexuals who might have come out of the world of "The Night of the Iguana," the third centers around a pitiful moron and her lecherous elderly professor, and the last is a moving portrayal of the disintegration of a lonely widow's ego.

[51] In such stories as "Torch Song" or "The Cure," both from *The Enormous Radio and Other Stories* (New York: Funk & Wagnalls, 1953).

[52] Dahl's two collections, both published by Knopf, are *Someone Like You* (1953) and *Kiss, Kiss* (1960); a kind of modern O. Henry with Freudian leanings, Dahl's characters include a little middle-aged lady with a penchant for embalming handsome youths, a wife who murders her husband with a frozen leg of lamb, and an immaculate little sadist who gambles for fingers. Dahl was born in Wales of Norwegian parents, but many of his stories were first published in America where he has lived in recent years.

[53] In, for example, "Success Story," a portrayal of the author of a successful first novel who becomes obsessed with the fear of death and eventually kills himself, or "Norman Allen," about a gifted Negro intellectual who commits suicide in a mental institution, both from *A Dangerous Woman and Other Stories* (New York: Vanguard, 1957).

[54] In *Pull Down Vanity and Other Stories* (Philadelphia: Lippincott, 1962), specifically in stories like "The Teeth" and "The Fear of Innocence," both of which contain grotesque characters who would be quite at home with Roderick and Madeline Usher.

[55] With humor and intelligence in individual stories and in *Heaven and Hardpan Farm* (New York: Scribner, 1957) a collection of stories originally published in *The New Yorker*, though billed by her publishers as a novel; the setting is a small private sanitarium presided over by an elderly psychiatrist whose eight female patients believe that Hardpan is the best of all possible sanitariums and that the Doctor himself is infallible.

Irwin Shaw,[59] I. B. Singer,[60] Gore Vidal,[61] and Edmund Wil-

---

[56] In *The Lottery or, the Adventures of James Harris* (New York: Farrar, Straus & Cudahy, 1949). The title story is said to have occasioned more letters to the editor than any story previously published in *The New Yorker*. Few recent writers can evoke the emotions of fear and surprise more successfully than Miss Jackson at her best, whether she is writing a parable-like fantasy of good and evil inherent in "law-abiding" citizens like "The Lottery," or whether she writes of prosaic individuals in an "ordinary" situation who suddenly become threatened with disaster as she does in the uncollected "The Summer People," originally published in *Charm* and included in Martha Foley's *The Best American Short Stories, 1951* (Boston: Houghton Mifflin, 1951). Mental illness is the subject of three of her novels: *The Road through the Woods* (1948), *Hangsaman* (1951), and *The Bird's Nest* (1954). *The Sundial* (1958), *The Haunting of Hill House* (1959), and *We Have Always Lived at the Castle* (1962) make effective use of the elements of horror, fantasy, and similar Gothic materials.

[57] In *A Commodity of Dreams and Other Stories* (New York: Simon and Schuster, 1959); Mr. Nemerov's characters include a crow-dynamiting recluse, a tourist-class Casanova who dances himself and his victim into the sea, and an old man who enjoys a deep-freeze afterlife.

[58] In *Vertical and Horizontal* (New York: Simon & Schuster, 1963), like *Heaven and Hardpan Farm* billed as a novel though originally appearing as a series of related *New Yorker* stories. The central characters are a New York internist and his analyst, Dr. Blauberman.

[59] In such a story as "The Climate of Insomnia," from *Mixed Company; Collected Short Stories of Irwin Shaw* (New York: Random House, 1950).

[60] In *Gimpel the Fool and Other Stories* (New York: Noonday, 1957) and *The Spinoza of Market Street* (New York: Farrar, Straus & Cudahy, 1961), both of which are commented on in Chapter Six, Part II.

[61] In *A Thirsty Evil. Seven Short Stories* (New York: Zero Press, 1956). Most of the characters in these stories pursue a thirsty evil to their ultimate destruction; like Shakespeare's rats (the title is from *Measure for Measure*) that "ravin down their proper bane," when they "do drink" they die. Michael and Mr. Royal of "Three Stratagems"

son[62] have in one way or other and with varying degrees of success concerned themselves with the fictional presentation of mental and emotional disturbance or with grotesque and Gothic materials. At the same time such lesser known writers as Uli Beigel,[63] Elisabeth Mann Borghese,[64] and the

---

are typical. Michael unconsciously equates marriage with death, sees his own "eventual downfall from beloved angel to deluded monster" but has neither will nor desire to resist. Mr. Royal, a widower infatuated with Michael, is a foreshadowing of what Michael himself will become. The collection with only one or two exceptions is a rather dreary landmark in the fictional presentation of homosexuality and the doomed search for self-realization, and displays little of the limited talent of Mr. Vidal's early novels.

[62] *Memoirs of Hecate County* (rev. ed.; New York: L. C. Page, 1959) in toto is a reflection upon societal and individual neuroses; Asa Stryker and Clarence Latouche of "The Man Who Shot Snapping Turtles," and Imogen Loomis, the truss-wearing princess of the novella "The Princess with the Golden Hair," could with some changes of accent and vocabulary be quite at home in the worlds of Jean Stafford or James Purdy.

[63] In *Victoria at Night and Other Stories* (New York: Random House, 1958), thirteen stories primarily concerned with women, Uli Beigel presents disturbed individuals who, like Miss Stafford's, are exiled from the world of healthy responses and relationships. Victoria of the title story wanders dazedly around Manhattan until dawn when she returns to the room in Morningside Heights where she had spent part of the night with a nameless young man. Another of Miss Beigel's agonizingly self-concerned young women searches desperately for "aloneness." Feeling that her lover has violated her inner identity, she commits suicide. Still another, a "gnawingly bored" schoolgirl, becomes nauseated at the "little, little things she was forced to be concerned about" and withdraws completely from reality. Miss Beigel's stories are knowledgeably and skillfully written, although her world is often vaguely defined and her characters tend to be abstractions rather than individuals.

[64] In *To Whom It May Concern* (New York: Braziller, 1960), Elisa-

late Charles Criswell [65] have published collections almost exclusively concerned with such materials.[66]

Louis Auchincloss's (1917–) *The Injustice Collectors* (1950), contains eight good stories of neurotic or disturbed characters who knowingly or unconsciously are seeking self-punishment or injustice. The term "injustice collector," as the author comments in his Introduction, is from Dr. Edmund Bergler's *The Battle for the Conscience,* and refers to individuals who unknowingly search for masochistic pleas-

---

beth Mann Borghese depicts a civilization sick and starving in the midst of technological plenty. In nine unusual and often bizarre stories, the daughter of the late Thomas Mann paints a nightmarish fantasy in which the individual has become an obsolescent experiment, a cipher in a world of untapped creative resources. The narrator of the title story, almost destroyed in the warfare between man and machine, offers to sell himself to the Inland Joy Development Corporation; a scientist, frozen in a daring experiment, is killed before he can record his experiences; in the best and most original story, "The Rehearsal," the members of a symphony orchestra mutilate themselves during a performance when their conductor, an ape, misses a figure on the score and runs amok.

[65] The dozen stories in Charles Criswell's (d. 1960) *Nobody Knows What the Stork Will Bring* (New York: McDowell, Obolensky, 1958) are concerned with madness, death, frustration, perversion, unhappy family relationships, and sad children. In "The Linden Tree" a mad woman reconstructs her past; in the title story a perverse child performs a chillingly indecent act upon her paralyzed grandfather; in "The Hobby" a dead father's collection of stamps and books turns out to be pornography. "Come In Come In," with its painfully realistic portrayal of a disorganized and frustrated young woman threatened by overwhelming evil, is reminiscent of Capote at his most effective.

[66] Outstanding among the large number of uncollected examples is Frank Butler's "To the Wilderness I Wander," originally in the *Hudson Review* and reprinted in Martha Foley's *Best American Short Stories, 1957* (Boston: Houghton Mifflin, 1957).

ure by creating situations in which they are mistreated or
disappointed. Characteristic is Gregory Bakewell of "Greg's
Peg," the most memorable story in this quietly effective collection. Greg is an amiable outsider, awkward and unlovable, a Mother's boy approaching thirty, and unmarried. The
story centers around Greg's efforts to become *accepted;*
eventually he manufactures a new personality, somewhat as
does Huxley's Theodore Gumbril, Jr., in *Antic Hay.* Greg
becomes a summer colony character, and an alcoholic buf-
foon. In a climactic scene a group of younger men become
irritated at his bizarre jig—Greg's Peg—and toss him into a
swimming pool. From that point on, Greg no longer can
claim the title of one of Anchor Harbor's social lions. De-
flated, he thinks of himself as "Poor Greg," quits his familiar
haunts, and subsequently dies of a heart attack.[67]

Loneliness dominates Sylvia Berkman's *Blackberry Wilderness* (1959), a collection of stories depicting with unassuming artistry and quiet understanding moments of crisis
in the lives of morbidly perceptive or over-fastidious characters. A worried American artist alone and friendless in
Rome, an acutely sensitive short story writer, an over-
fastidious proofreader who becomes involved in an act of
sudden violence—for all their intelligence, or perhaps partly
because of their intelligence, these people move through life
like somnambulists. Engaged in essentially meaningless activity or frightened by nameless fears, they come in contact
with other human beings only briefly, before their dread of

[67] *The Injustice Collectors* (Boston: Houghton Mifflin, 1950) is Mr.
Auchincloss's second book but the first published under his own name;
it is characterized generally by the wit and urbanity of his subsequent
fiction which has earned him considerable praise as a mid-century
Jamesian.

"involvement" forces them to retreat. The story of their lives is the story of unfulfilled moments, gambits refused, love denied, or the rejection of someone's need.

"Which is delusion, which is real?—Festival or blackberry wilderness?" [68] This is the dilemma which confronts Miss Berkman's unhappy people who are often unable to distinguish between external reality and the inner world of personal visions. Like Madeleine, the career woman of "Pippa Passes," they yearn to establish contact with their fellows, but fear forces them to remain isolated, contemplating the world as Madeleine contemplates her fellow travelers on a New York to Paris flight:

> Turning, she scanned the faces of the other passengers. Who escaped? Strip any one of them down and you'd find a hidden mutilated segment too—a nerve center choked, a muscle stunted, a capacity blocked. That was why she and her New York . . . friends walked so warily. They were afraid because they were ashamed, and ashamed because they were scarred.[69]

Although some of Miss Berkman's characters, like Beatrice Ransome of the title story, find a kind of salvation through art, only occasionally do they dare, with the discarded wife of "October Journey," to invade the realms of despair and survive to say, "This journey into alien land is over. I am ready now. I am ready to go back." [70]

---

[68] Sylvia Berkman, "Blackberry Wilderness," *Blackberry Wilderness* (New York: Doubleday, 1959), p. 150.

[69] "Pippa Passes," p. 101.

[70] "October Journey," p. 239. Some of these comments originally appeared in my "Sleepwalking through Life," *New York Times Book Review* (Jan. 15, 1959), p. 5.

Except for the stories of Tennessee Williams, perhaps the most extreme use of grotesque and violent materials in contemporary short fiction is seen in Paul Bowles's (1911–) *The Delicate Prey and Other Stories* (1950), dedicated "for my mother, who first read me the stories of Poe." In some of the seventeen *Delicate Prey* pieces, the author's seriousness of intent is more questionable than his very palpable talent. Many of these stories are reminiscent of Poe at his worst, which was often, rather than his best, and Mr. Bowles frequently writes like a precocious child who read Monk Lewis and Krafft-Ebing too young and had not quite recovered from the experience at the time of writing these stories.

The title story, for example, contains several murders, sodomy, emasculation, and insanity. "By the Water" presents a young North African traveler who is threatened by monsters both human and crustacean. In "A Distant Episode" a professor, captured by a tribe in "the warm country" who remove successively both his tongue and his reason, runs madly through the countryside, dressed in tin. "You Are Not I," one of the two stories with an American locale, introduces us to a crazy girl who drops stones into the mouths of corpses. In "The Circular Valley," a spirit which inhabits an abandoned monastery takes possession of male and female alike, including an adulterous couple, the male member of which eventually falls off a cliff.

Such wholehearted immersions into a bloodbath of horror and violence are individually arresting, usually carry the impact of a violent kick in the groin, and at their best effectively suggest, as do the stories of Tennessee Williams, that beneath our "sophisticated" and enlightened society we are lost voyagers in a bleak and uncharted desert. Too often, though, it seems that Mr. Bowles so enthusiastically flogs the dead horse of horror for its own sake as to render ex-

tremely questionable a recent conclusion that most of the
Delicate Prey stories are "highly moral tales." [71] Impressive
one or two at a time, Mr. Bowles's stories collectively tend to
leave me with an impression akin to that produced by a visit
to a chamber of horrors. After the first swift shock, the blood
on the mutilated corpses is seen to be red paint, and the
accumulation of violence and terror eventually produces little more than apathy or disgust.[72]

Truman Capote's (1924–) spectacular literary career began in the middle forties with the publication of two strange
and eerie tales, "A Tree of Night" and "Miriam," which are
characteristic of his first collection of short fiction, published in 1949, *A Tree of Night and Other Stories.* These
early stories are an effective mingling of psychological insight and the familiar materials and themes of the horror
story. Gothic extravagance, madness, sensationalism, the supernatural, and the surreal permeate them, but at their
best they are contemporary classics of the genre, remarkable in their totality of effect, and executed with virtuosity
and technical adroitness.[73]

[71] Oliver Evans, "Paul Bowles and the 'Natural' Man," *Recent American Fiction; Some Critical Views,* ed. Joseph J. Waldmeir (Boston:
Houghton Mifflin, 1963), p. 143.
[72] Some of these comments originally appeared in my "Extreme Personalities," *New Republic* (March 26, 1951), p. 20. A later collection, *A Hundred Camels in the Courtyard* (San Francisco: City Lights
Books, 1962), contains four stories of Moslems in North Africa. They
possess in common an apparently perceptive understanding of "life
among the natives" and are concerned with violence, sorcery, and
hashish: " 'A pipe of Kif before breakfast gives a man the strength of
a hundred camels in the courtyard.' " ("He of the Assembly," p. 38.)
[73] Various critics have commented on the marked contrast between
the "nocturnal" tone of most of the *A Tree of Night* stories and the
"daylight" tone of such pieces as "My Side of the Matter" and "Jug
of Silver." The same contrast exists between the title novella and the

The title story is characteristic. Kay, a young woman traveling alone by train, is set upon by a female dwarf with an oversized melon of a head (freaks of one sort or another appear and reappear in Capote's stories with about the same frequency as they do in Poe's) and her male companion, a cadaverous cretin (he has "queer" eyes, wears a Mickey Mouse watch, and has "anointed himself with a cheap, vile perfume") who formerly made his living by being buried alive in carnival sideshows. As the rickety train creaks and groans its way through the Alabama night, the strange couple slowly cast a spell over Kay; she wants to "cry out and waken everyone in the coach," but is unable to do so. As she gazes somnambulistically at the pale-eyed man, his face seems "to change form and recede before her like a moon-shaped rock sliding downward under a surface of water. A warm laziness relaxed her. She was dimly conscious of it when the woman took away her purse, and when she gently pulled the raincoat like a shroud over her head." [74]

The same nightmarish quality animates several of Capote's stories including "Miriam," in which a middle-aged woman, Mrs. Miller, is besieged by a strange child; the surrealistic "The Headless Hawk"; "Master Misery," with its somber conflict between the world of dreams and external reality; and "Shut a Final Door," with its compelling depiction of individual disintegration. In such stories Capote has created a

---

three stories of *Breakfast at Tiffany's* (New York: Random House, 1958), particularly "A Christmas Memory," which is a sunny and warmhearted recollection of an ingenuous boy and his grandmother. Ihab Hassan has commented perceptively on this in "Truman Capote: the Vanishing Image of Narcissus," *Radical Innocence; Studies in the Contemporary American Novel* (Princeton: Princeton Univ. Press, 1961), pp. 230–58.

[74] Truman Capote, "A Tree of Night," *A Tree of Night and Other Stories* (New York: Random House, 1949), p. 209.

universe of opposites—of daily vision contrasted with the vision of nightmare and delirium, of light and darkness, of accustomed reality as opposed to myth or romance. Capote's victims are trapped in this world, as Coleridge's Christabel is trapped, to become apathetic or helpless witnesses to their own destruction by the forces of the dark, at the hands of devil child or wizard man, or by projections of their inner weaknesses or fears. Like Walter of "Shut a Final Door," shivering and vomiting and falling to pieces physically and emotionally in a New Orleans hotel, most of the people in these "dark" stories are "awfully alone in this world." All their acts are "acts of fear," and fear and loneliness destroy them as thoroughly as Walter is destroyed.[75]

In William Goyen's (1915–) first collection of short stories, *Ghost and Flesh* (1952), the nature of reality is depicted in terms of a never-ceasing conflict between the present and the past, between the visible and the invisible. Goyen presents this conflict with considerable variety of mood, method, and subject matter. In the essentially realistic "The White Rooster," Grandpa Samuels kills the young woman who is planning to kill a stray rooster which has caught his fancy; in the grotesque and masquelike "The Grasshopper's Burden," a monster of a child, seated on the King's Throne in a burning schoolhouse, strikes terror to the soul of the narrator; in the fantasy "A Shape of Light" an eccentric widower, Boney Benson, like a skeleton-headed ghost on a purple horse pursues a distorted vision of reality.

These and other characters are dominated or victimized by what the author seems to consider the tyrannies of the past, of tradition, of sex, and of an all-encompassing, nameless fear. They search for a means of effecting some kind of

[75] "Shut a Final Door," pp. 88, 75.

satisfactory compromise between past and present; they struggle to believe that life and death, the visible and the invisible, are factors in a continuous chain of being which is existence.

" 'Us humans are part ghost and part flesh,' " the central character of "Ghost and Flesh, Water and Dirt" concludes, " 'but I think maybe the ghost part is the longest lastin . . . there's a world both places, a world where there's ghosts and a world where there's flesh, and I believe the real right way is to take our worlds, of ghost or of flesh . . . as they come and take what comes in em . . . and be what each . . . wants us to be.' " [76]

In spite of Goyen's cloudy metaphysics, florid rhetoric, and emotional intensity which at times approximates hysteria, *Ghost and Flesh* is a memorable book. Like his first novel, *The House of Breath,* its very excesses indicated a real, if youthful, talent. The promise of this collection was fulfilled in his later stories, collected as *Faces of Blood Kindred* in 1960. Goyen here remains concerned with the relationship between the past and the present, between the living and the dead, but his more recent stories are purged of the Gothic excesses of their predecessors. Only the novella, "A Tale of Inheritance," is close kin to *Ghost and Flesh.* This fable of the bearded Lester sisters—"One time were two sisters in a faraway county of Texas . . . and they had little black beards" [77]—is both impressive and irritating. It is marred by an overelaborate concern for language and technique at the expense of clarity of vision.

---

[76] William Goyen, "Ghost and Flesh," *Ghost and Flesh; Stories and Tales* (New York: Random House, 1952), p. 89. I have expressed some of these ideas in "The Lower Depths," *Saturday Review* (March 22, 1952), p. 17.

[77] William Goyen, "A Tale of Inheritance," *The Faces of Blood Kindred* (New York: Random House, 1960), p. 105.

Many of the best stories of Charles Jackson (1903–) are concerned with the slow but steady emotional or intellectual disintegration of fundamentally decent human beings who, like Louis Auchincloss's "injustice collectors," are their own worst enemies. The title story of his first collection, *The Sunnier Side* (1950), was certainly one of the best stories of that year or of recent years although it was ignored by the editors of the *Best* and *O. Henry* volumes. Violating just about every known taboo of mass circulation magazine fiction, and one or two taboos until then undiscovered, "The Sunnier Side" is part essay on the nature of short story writing and part re-creation of the lives of four "nice" girls from an upstate New York small town, "Arcadia," during the middle of the second decade.[78] Narrated in retrospect by a writer who was a small boy when the girls were teenagers, the story is both a compassionate and ironic commentary on the sad gap between the dreams of youth and the uncompromising realities of adulthood. Death, violence, or shame are the destiny of the four "nice girls" whom the narrator, even after all the shocking revelations of their adulthood, remembers as "Campfire Girls, paddling earnestly . . . along the bay in twin canoes . . . hair parted in the middle and hanging straight . . . on all sides, long below your shoulders, bound with a beaded bandeau . . . I can still hear your Campfire cry, 'Wo-he-lo!'—and the words of the song that went with it:

"'Wo-he-lo for work, Wo-he-lo for health, Wo-he-lo . . . for love . . .'"[79]

The same blending of compassion and irony, affection

---

[78] The story, despite its taboos and to the credit of the editors who accepted it, originally appeared in *Cosmopolitan*.

[79] Charles Jackson, "The Sunnier Side," *The Sunnier Side; Twelve Arcadian Tales* (New York: Farrar, Straus, 1950), pp. 73–74.

and disgust, characterizes Mr. Jackson's second collection, *Earthly Creatures* (1953). The central character of most of these stories is his own worst enemy. He appears in many forms, as adolescent boy, young woman, middle-aged novelist, or elderly mother. Something has gone wrong in his life or is in the process of going wrong. In an agony of self-indulgence or self-pity, he lashes out at things as they are. In story after story, he methodically goes about the business of destroying himself.

Like the schizophrenic non-hero of the best story in the collection, "The Boy Who Ran Away," Mr. Jackson's people are worthy of the love or understanding they need so desperately and seek with such futility. The narrator of "The Boy Who Ran Away," for example, hates his gawky nephew for the very traits which had made his own childhood unhappy. When the nephew breaks the gift the narrator's daughters gave him for Christmas, the awkward boy sets in progress an unhappy chain of events. The father deprives his children of their anticipated New Year's Eve pleasure and hates himself for it yet is powerless to do more than resort to additional whiskey and his ever-present seconal. He is chained with bonds of his own forging, forever tearing at the exposed viscera of his own self-respect. In effect, he feels he has abdicated life: "he was finished, through, done for, as finally as if God had come into the room and beckoned him with the ultimate finger. He was ridden with fear, guilt, and self-disgust. . . . He was his own devil, his own black beast. . . . He hated himself with an active hatred that was almost too much for a single human body to contain . . . and he did not think he could contain that hatred another hour." [80]

[80] Charles Jackson, "The Boy Who Ran Away," *Earthly Creatures; Ten Stories* (New York: Farrar, Straus & Young, 1953), pp. 36–37. Some

To say that Carson McCullers (1917–) possesses a fondness for the Gothic is but to note, as has been observed, "and note superficially, her interest in the grotesque, the freakish, and the incongruous."[81] "The Ballad of the Sad Cafe" amply underscores the generalization. Miss Amelia, a six-foot virgin bootlegger with a face "like the terrible dim faces known in dreams, sexless and white,"[82] has lived for years isolated in a decaying, boarded-up, swaybacked house in a "dreary" Southern town. Marvin Macy, her husband, is as strong, dark, and sinister as any Gothic hero in English or American literature; it is rumored that he carries with him the ear of a man he had once killed in a razor fight. Prior to the actual time span of the novella, Marvin and Miss Amelia have been married, a marriage never consummated, and Marvin leaves town after being humiliated by Miss Amelia. A decade after this departure, a hideous dwarf, Lyman, appears upon the scene, claims to be kin to Miss Amelia, drinks her corn liquor, and effectively courts her.[83] Marvin Macy

---

of these comments originally appeared in my "Self-Destructors," *Saturday Review* (Oct. 10, 1953), pp. 17–18. Following the success and notoriety of his first novel, *The Lost Weekend* (1944), and the Ray Milland motion picture version of it, Jackson's reputation declined, although he published two good novels in addition to his short stories, *The Fall of Valor* (1946) and *The Outer Edges* (1948). Except for *The Lost Weekend* his best work is in the short story; he is an undervalued, underestimated writer.

[81] Ihab Hassan, "Carson McCullers: The Aesthetics of Love and Pain," *Radical Innocence*, p. 207.

[82] "The Ballad of the Sad Cafe," *The Ballad of the Sad Cafe. The Novels and Stories of Carson McCullers* (Boston: Houghton Mifflin, 1951), p. 3.

[83] Lyman was "scarcely more than four feet tall, and he wore a ragged, dusty coat. . . . His crooked little legs seemed too thin to carry the

returns shortly thereafter, and in terms of this grotesque, obscene triangle Mrs. McCullers creates a compelling and nightmarish parable of love which is not love and human relations which are anti-human in their thick and clotted perversity. The "Ballad" reaches its peak in perhaps the most grotesque of all grotesque climaxes, a fantastic Ground Hog Day tournament between Miss Amelia and Marvin Macy, a wrestling match which becomes strictly no contest when Lyman enters the fray.

Though few of Mrs. McCullers's people are as grotesquely memorable as Miss Amelia, Macy, and Lyman, they share with them the fact that they are failures or outcasts in a world in which traditional values are reversed or almost unrecognizable. They include a jockey who is on the skids, a music student who is losing her technique, a writer who can no longer write, a foreign correspondent who is perpetually an exile and an alien, and a once-brilliant teacher who has become a pathological liar. Meaningless or ungratifying or distorted love, loneliness, and decay are dominant elements in the worlds of these unhappy misfits.

Flannery O'Connor (1925–) has more and more clearly emerged as the most gifted and most likely to endure Southern woman writer since Eudora Welty, and *A Good Man Is Hard to Find and Other Stories* (1955), her second book of fiction but her only published collection of short stories, is perhaps the most memorable first book of short

---

weight of his great warped chest and the hump that sat on his shoulders. He had a very large head, with deep-set blue eyes and a sharp little mouth. His face was both soft and sassy—at the moment his pale skin was yellowed by dust and there were lavender shadows beneath his eyes." (*Ibid.*, p. 6.)

fiction since Eudora Welty's *A Curtain of Green*. Since *A Good Man Is Hard To Find*, Miss O'Connor's talent has deepened and widened; her second novel and such recent shorter pieces as "Greenleaf," "Comforts of Home," "Everything That Rises Must Converge," and the novella "The Lame Shall Enter First" are among her best work.[84]

The world of *A Good Man Is Hard to Find* is the author's native South, for the most part peopled by poor, rural characters usually depicted in unusual or bizarre situations and deeply influenced by individual or societal attitudes, antipathies, or paradoxes. Central to Miss O'Connor's effectiveness is her creation of a remarkable gallery of misfits, rejects, or grotesques—young and old, black and white, vain and humble. Within her sharply etched landscapes, and frequently in terms of an outlandish humor which is robust, sardonic, and sick by turns, these characters assume monstrous life, from wooden-legged Hulga of "Good Country People" and her Bible-toting lover who wants to add her wooden leg to his collection of pornography and glass eyes, to the narcissistic Mrs. Shortley of "The Displaced Person," the violent sons of "A Circle in the Fire," Grandma Bailey of the title story, shot three times by the Misfit, and the hermaphrodite of "A Temple of the Holy Ghost."

The effective juxtaposition of opposites previously commented on is the source of much of Flannery O'Connor's

[84] "Greenleaf" was first published in the *Kenyon Review* and is first-prize winner in the 1941 *Prize Stories,* ed. Paul Engle and Constance Urdang (New York: Doubleday, 1957); "Comforts of Home" was published in the *Kenyon Review* (Fall 1960); "Everything that Rises Must Converge," originally appeared in *New World Writing* and is included in *The Best American Short Stories, 1962,* ed. Martha Foley and David Burnett (Boston: Houghton Mifflin, 1962); "The Lame Shall Enter First" was published in the *Sewanee Review* (Summer 1962).

power. Her work is a curious mixture of love and cruelty, of
the comic and the serious and the tragic. In her illuminating
"The Fiction Writer and His Country," Miss O'Connor has
said that "writers who see by the light of their Christian faith
will have, in these times, the sharpest eyes for the grotesque,
for the perverse, and for the unacceptable." [85] The comment
has disturbed some of her critics, who find her belief in essentially orthodox and traditional religious values incom-
patible with her "black humor" and her preoccupation with
violence and abnormality. The paradoxical character of her
work is less confusing, however, when one recalls the number
of the lame, the halt, and the blind, the freaks, misfits,
grotesques, and societal rejects of the New Testament. In
this light, it is possible to accept at face value Miss O'Connor's belief that in the greatest fiction a writer's "moral sense
coincides with his dramatic sense," [86] nor does it come as any
great shock when we are told that she thinks she "would admit" to writing "what Hawthorne called 'romances'" and
that she feels "more of a kinship with Hawthorne than with
any other American writer." [87]

Miss O'Connor, in short, is basically an allegorist or fan-
tasist rather than a realist, although her stories are so securely rooted in specific time and place as to seem as real as
rain. She is in the highest sense a moralist working out of a
preconceived dogma, not a journalist or a scavenger fum-
bling with Gothic horrors and monstrosities for their sakes.

[85] Flannery O'Connor, "The Fiction Writer and His Country," in *The
Living Novel: A Symposium,* ed. Granville Hicks (New York: Macmillan, 1957), p. 162.

[86] *Ibid.,* 161.

[87] Quoted from a letter from Miss O'Connor to John Hawkes in his
perceptive article, "Flannery O'Connor's Devil," *Sewanee Review*
(Summer 1962), p. 395.

Again like Hawthorne, who at his best shared Miss O'Connor's fondness for the abnormal and the diseased and the bizarre, her eye is both upon this world and the next. The fault of her characters, she suggests, is primarily in themselves, precipitated by societal and hereditary flaws, not solely in their stars. Through arrogance, self-sufficiency, stupidity, or worst of all pride, her people have attempted to find their own salvation—even their groping, inchoate search for love is primarily narcissistic, as Irving Malin has pointed out—and in so doing have committed the cardinal sin of rejecting the redemptive function of Christianity.[88]

The reasons for the recent fiction writer's concern with mental illness and the grotesque are many and varied. The influence of Freud and a corresponding growing concern for the emotional complexities of the human experience; the revolt from tradition and the spiraling of tensions in a changing society; World War II and its aftermath; the loss of individualism in an authority-dominated culture—these and many other factors have been suggested as explanations for the ever-growing body of contemporary sick fiction. Whatever its causes, this is a literature of striking contrasts, opposites, and paradox. It is a merging of the serious and the ludicrous, the meaningful and the meaningless, the beautiful and the ugly, the noble and the ignoble. This sick literature is preoccupied with the non-hero's or the anti-hero's often

[88] Among many recent discussions of Flannery O'Connor's short stories, see Irving Malin's *New America Gothic,* pp. 36–38; 62–67; 92–95; 120–24; 143–45. For Miss O'Connor, a Catholic, there is nothing further from the truth than the belief that "Christian dogma is a hindrance to the writer." See her "The Fiction Writer and His Country," and "Church and the Fiction Writer," *America* (March 30, 1957), pp. 733–35.

frantic search for self, or his passive retreat into isolation or abnormality as perhaps the last defense against a society or a concept of life which he considers ridiculous, meaningless, or destructive. Its recurrent themes and subjects include man's capacity for self-destruction, his propensity for failure, his inability to communicate meaningfully with others; loneliness and violence, human waste and deterioration, abnormality and perversion appear and reappear in it. It is a literature almost unrelievedly somber in which in the final analysis, as Tennessee Williams has phrased it, "the earth destroys her crooked child." [89]

[89] Nelson, *Tennessee Williams,* p. 97.

6. Of War and Peace
and Other Matters

I. *The War and the Short Story*

WORLD WAR II, it has often been observed, was the most fully recorded disaster in the history of the world. In addition to the miles of official records, tons of newspaper dispatches, and truckloads of histories, biographies, and reminiscences of a multitude of individuals ranging from chiefs-of-staff to cooks and stenographers, World War II and the Korean War provided subject and theme for a mass of short fiction. Hundreds and hundreds of so-called "war" stories appeared in American magazines from 1941 to 1946, the great majority of them jerry-built to satisfy a well-fed civilian populace's craving for fiction concerning characters

and events "out there" or "overseas." This avalanche of
mediocrity was little more than an opportunistic transfor-
mation of the pulp or slick story of the immediate past.
Military installations, theaters of operation, rest camps, *et al.*
replaced the Western cattle town, the big-city apartment, or
the athletic field; and the sheriff or athlete turned up in
sergeant's stripes or lieutenant's bars. The golden-haired girl
in the rose-covered cottage or the erring young wife under-
went similar transformations, and emerged as WAC, WAVE,
USO entertainer, or Rosie the Riveter.

Almost buried in this quagmire, however, are many good
individual war stories and a small handful of notable collections of short stories. Except for *Tales of the South Pacific,*
most of these have been forgotten along with the slush of
the popular magazines.[1] The best of them, however, are
among the best short fiction of the last two decades.

The best single collection of stories about World War II is
John Horne Burns's (1916–1953) *The Gallery* (1947), if this
powerful series of what the author terms "promenades"
and "portraits" of American military personnel and Italian
civilians whose lives cross in and around the Galleria Umberto
in Naples during the late summer of 1944 can be called a
collection of stories rather than a novel. John Burns was a
major talent. He wrote with gusto, prodigality, and energy
reminiscent of Thomas Wolfe. Like Wolfe he was expert in
re-creating the essence of places and people; his pictures of

---

[1] Some good stories, almost without exception by older non-partici-
pants, appeared in the mass circulation magazines, notably Stephen
Vincent Benét's "A Judgment in the Mountains," William Faulkner's
"Two Soldiers," and Paul Gallico's "The Snow Goose" (the first in
Country Gentleman, the second and third in the *Saturday Evening
Post*), but for the most part popular magazine short stories about the
war were hurried, slick, and formularized.

wartime Casablanca and Algiers and Naples are unforgettable and, according to those who were there at approximately the same times, more real than any documentary ever could be. At the same time, Burns was a fine reporter with a great ear for dialogue and an attitude toward human misery compounded of skepticism, despair, and affection which reminds one, as do so many of the younger war writers, of Hemingway. But Burns was not just another talented young imitator. He was a fresh, powerful, and essentially independent genius, and his early death, in Italy where he was working on a novel, was a disaster. *The Gallery,* as some contemporary book reviewers were quick to point out (and to overemphasize), is an uneven book. It is too sentimental toward the Italians, too repetitious in its concern with sex, too clinical in its depiction, say, of the one hundred and eighty hours in the life of an American sergeant confined to the venereal disease ward of a Naples hospital.[2] All this is true, but only to a degree. *The Gallery* is a big book, big in concept and big in achievement. As uncompromisingly realistic as a death certificate, only rarely do its characters get bogged down in detail, and in the final analysis it is full of vitality and life, and rich in compassion and understanding.

Next to *The Gallery,* Robert Lowry's (1919–) *The Wolf That Fed Us* (1949,), seems to me the best short story collection directly concerned with World War II. The stories range in time from the beginning of the war to its aftermath; their settings include New York, San Francisco, El Paso, and Rome during the Allied Occupation. Collectively, they lack the total impact of *The Gallery* and the sweep and lyrical intensity of Burns's stories. Like Burns, on the other

[2] John Horne Burns, "Eighth Portrait: Queen Penicillin," *The Gallery* (New York: Harper, 1947).

hand, Lowry is an expert reporter and a compassionate observer of people and places and events. At his best, as he is in "Layover in El Paso" or the title story with its detailed depiction of American infantrymen in newly occupied Rome, Lowry captures the essence of characters at a specific time in history with an accurate understanding which more than compensates for his occasional repetition of mood and incident. The lonely wife of "Layover in El Paso," for example, is described in only two lines, and then immediately fades out of the story, never to reappear, but in those two lines she comes to life completely, both as an individual and as a type.[3] Such stories transcend reportage by the author's constant ability to suggest the universal in terms of the specific. Lowry's angry, sad, fleabitten stories and their likable, often ingenuous men in and out of uniform are part of the history of our times.

If *The Gallery* is the best collection of short stories about World War II, James Michener's (1907–) *Tales of the South Pacific* (1947) is unquestionably the most popular; as best-selling book, musical drama, and motion picture it is one of the phenomena of recent entertainment history. Michener's popularity is understandable. He tells a tale well, whether it be a pleasantly gossipy anecdote about what happened to the zipper on Admiral Kester's trousers, recollections of a conversation with the aged daughter of Fletcher Christian, or a more dramatic and traditionally plotted story

[3] "Who cares! says the lonely wife returning from visiting her husband for the last time before overseas duty. She holds hands with two soldiers she never saw before, and she has starry eyes and a short skirt, and helps kill a pint on the platform." (Robert Lowry, "Layover in El Paso," *The Wolf That Fed Us* [New York: Doubleday, 1949, p. 35].)

like "The Airstrip at Konora." Michener demands little of the reader; his stories are like a pleasant exchange between friends over cigars and brandy. He satisfies his readers' desire for apparently authentic information about the faraway places of romance, and gives them at the same time tidbits of information and legend or the stuff out of which legend is made. Perhaps most central to his enormous popularity, however, is his timeliness, his flair for contemporaneity. Beneath the casual air, the relaxed method, and the ingratiating manner of a nice-guy narrator, the reader is constantly made aware of the faint pulsations of history in the making—Guadalcanal, the Coral Sea, the last great battles of the Navy Line. Tragedy and violence appear in *Tales of the South Pacific* occasionally, such as the death of Commander Hoag at the suicidal hands of a "screaming, wild, disheveled" Japanese, "his eyes popping from his horrible head, this primitive indecent thing," [4] but for the most part Michener paints a not unpleasant picture. His officers, as the late Charles Fenton observed, are "gentlemen all . . . in the old romantic tradition" [5] and theirs is the kind of war about which a mother, daughter, wife, or fiancée might hope, if *he* has to go, pray let it be like this.

Other notable collections of war stories include Kay Boyle's (1903–) *The Smoking Mountain; Stories of Postwar Germany* (1951), an often effective blending of reportage

[4] James A. Michener, "The Airstrip at Konora," *Tales of the South Pacific* (New York: Macmillan, 1947), p. 255.
[5] Charles A. Fenton, Introduction, *The Best Short Stories of World War II: An American Anthology* (New York: Viking, 1957), p. xix. This is no run-of-the-mill introduction to just another anthology. Fenton has written a knowledgeable, perceptive essay, unquestionably the best of its kind I have read. His comments on his individual selections are equally good.

and fiction, and memorable in its delineation of the contrast between conqueror and conquered in an occupied country.[6]

Christopher La Farge's (1897–1956) *East by Southwest* (1944) consists of ten stories, uneven in quality but at their best moving and unpretentious, and a poem, about American military personnel in a remote battle area in the South Pacific, observed when La Farge covered this theater as a correspondent for *Harper's*.[7]

Robert McLaughlin's (1908–) *A Short Wait Between Trains* (1945) contains eighteen brief stories of army life from basic training in Alabama, "Basic Soldier," to combat in New Guinea, "Unopposed Landing." Most of the stories are set in the United States and many of them, like "Poor Everybody," are concerned with contrasts between military and civilian life.[8]

Edward Newhouse's (1911–) *The Iron Chain* (1946) is similar to *A Short Wait Between Trains* in its concern with the periphery of war, rather than war itself, and is set for the most part in or around New York.[9]

Robert Shaplen's *A Corner of the World* (1946) consists

[6] Many of Kay Boyle's best known stories prior to *The Smoking Mountain* are collected in *Thirty Stories* (New York: Simon & Schuster, 1946) which includes thirteen published in 1940 or later which are concerned with the prelude to World War II or the war itself, among them "Defeat," which received first prize in the 1941 *Prize Stories*, ed. Herschel Brickell (New York: Doubleday, Doran, 1941).
[7] *East by Southwest* was published by Coward-McCann, 1944.
[8] Robert McLaughlin, *A Short Wait Between Trains and Other Stories* (New York: Knopf, 1945).
[9] Many of the stories in Edward Newhouse's last collection, *Many Are Called: Forty-Two Short Stories* (New York: Sloane, 1951) are similarly concerned with war; two of the *Iron Chain* stories are also reprinted here.

of one short and four long stories all preoccupied with the aftermath of war; they involve Americans, transplanted Europeans, and Asiatics in Shanghai, India, Saigon, Manila, and Macao.[10]

Bert Stiles's (1920–1944) *Serenade to the Big Bird* (1952) is somewhat reminiscent of William March's World War I classic, *Company K.* Terse, simple, and often moving sketches of combat and the author's reaction to it, together with Stiles's reminiscences of the past and "a doll named August" and his hopes for the future, *Serenade* is the work of a very talented young author. Stiles's death while flying escort on a bombing raid in the autumn of 1944 was a tragedy in more ways than one.[11]

Though none of Irwin Shaw's (1913–) several collections of short stories is exclusively concerned with the War, his war stories are among his best known and most successful work. "Sailor off the Bremen" is an engrossing, if ideologically confusing, mixture of suspense, violence, and political commentary narrated in terms of a Nazi steward, a Communist deck officer, and two sharply contrasted American brothers. In "Gunner's Passage," perhaps Shaw's best story, three American enlisted men at an Air Force base in North Africa talk and think about their past experiences and what the future holds in store for them; it is a work eloquent in its simplicity, and revealing in its understanding of uncomplicated men of goodwill in a world of violence. "Walking Wounded," a character study of the disintegration of a British officer confined to a desk job in Egypt after years of combat, was the first-prize winner in the 1944 *Prize Stories.* "Act of Faith" is a kind of parable which contrasts racial intoler-

[10] Robert Shaplen, *A Corner of the World* (New York: Knopf, 1949).
[11] Bert Stiles, *Serenade to the Big Bird* (New York: Norton, 1952).

ance and goodwill; it is adroitly and often movingly built around three American combat infantrymen, including a Jew who has just received from his father a terrifying letter concerning anti-Semitism in America. "The City Was in Total Darkness" depicts a successful novelist with prewar jitters, whose trip to Tia Juana with a party girl is climaxed by the news that England has just declared war on Germany. "The Passion of Lance Corporal Hawkins" is a story of sadism and the persecution of the Jews, and in "Hamlets of the World" a group of French soldiers kill their commanding officer whose fate suggests one aspect of the tragedy of modern France. Other Shaw stories concerned with war or its aftermath include "The Priest," "The Man with One Arm," "Medal from Jerusalem," "Preach the Dusty Roads," and "Tip on a Dead Jockey." [12]

Although Shaw is a first-class journalist, a marvelously adroit fiction writer, and man of goodwill, even some of his best stories, like "Act of Faith," seem over-contrived and over-manipulated when read in an emotional or sociological climate different from that in which they were written. His later stories, collected in *Tip on a Dead Jockey* (1957), are a decided letdown, and Shaw's shortcomings—his contrivance, glibness, superficiality, sentimentality, and too-clever card-stacking—are more apparent now than they were when his fiction was concerned with the larger problems of international politics, war, and racial injustice.

J. D. Salinger's (1919–) war stories are not concerned with the actual depiction of war but with its effects upon participants and non-participants alike. "For Esmé—With Love

[12] Except for "Tip on a Dead Jockey," from *Tip on a Dead Jockey and Other Stories* (New York: Random House, 1957), all of these stories are available in *Mixed Company; Collected Stories of Irwin Shaw* (New York: Random House, 1950).

and Squalor," "A Perfect Day for Bananafish," and "Uncle Wiggily in Connecticut" are contemporary classics. Each of these highly individualistic stories is concerned with a different kind of casualty of war: "Esmé" with its fresh and vivid characterizations of a precocious English girl whose father "was s-l-a-i-n in North Africa" and an American infantryman; "A Perfect Day," with its equally memorable portrayal of the amiable and gentle Seymour Glass, the suicide who has become the central figure in Salinger's hierarchy of saints;[13] and "Uncle Wiggily" with its civilian casualty, if the likable young mother whose lover had been killed during the war can be so designated. Each of these stories is alive with the warmhearted understanding and lightness of touch of Salinger at his very best, yet each beneath its surface is bleak and tragic. Few writers can manipulate these contrasts more adroitly and more meaningfully than Salinger, just as few writers have been able to ring more successive changes on the recurring thesis, central to almost all of Salinger's work, both short and long, of the need for love and understanding, without which life becomes unbearable or meaningless—a "perfect day for bananafish," but not for human beings.

The list of individual memorable war stories is varied and extensive; bearing in mind Herschel Brickell's statement that the short story is a "perfect subject for argument and honest difference of opinion," [14] here are a few of them. Robert O. Bowen's (1920–) "A Matter of Price," a sympa-

[13] Tom Davis argues persuasively that Sergeant X of "Esmé" and Seymour Glass of "Bananafish" are one and the same, in "J. D. Salinger: the Identity of Sergeant X," *The Western Humanities Review* (Spring 1962), pp. 181–83.
[14] Herschel Brickell, Introduction, *Prize Stories of 1942* (New York: Doubleday, Doran, 1942), p. xv.

thetic characterization of a Korean war casualty confronted
with the mental castration of a lobotomy;[15] Eugene Burdick's
(1918–) first published story, "Rest Camp on Maui," a dev-
astating if contrived portrayal of a glib war correspondent
who would be quite at home in the pages of *The Ugly American;*[16] Laurence Critchell's (1917–) "Flesh and Blood," another effective first story, about an American lieutenant's
"infidelity" in wartime England, a sympathetic and restrained picture of men without women which evoked considerable foolish criticism when it first appeared in the *Atlantic;*[17] Daniel B. Dodson's (1918–) "The Let-Down," a gripping narrative of an American mission over the Himalayas;[18]
Harris Downey's "The Hunted," about a day in the life of
a combat infantryman separated from his platoon in France,
a lost man, debased and bewildered by fatigue and destruction;[19] George Garrett's (1929–) 'The Old Army Game," a
freshly individualistic treatment of basic training;[20] Martha
Gellhorn's (1908–) "For Better, for Worse" and "Till Death
Do Us Part," the first about an Italian nobleman who serves

[15] Robert Bowen, "A Matter of Price," *Marlow the Master and Other
Stories* (Northport, Alabama: Colonial Press, 1963).

[16] Originally published in *Harper's,* "Rest Camp on Maui" was the
second-prize winner in the 1947 *Prize Stories,* ed. Herschel Brickell
(New York: Doubleday, 1947).

[17] "Flesh and Blood" received the prize for the best "first" story in
the 1945 *Prize Stories,* ed. Herschell Brickell (New York: Doubleday,
1945).

[18] Daniel B. Dodson, "The Let-Down," *Story: The Magazine of the
Short Story in Book Form, Number One,* ed. Whit Burnett and Hallie
Burnett (New York: McKay, 1951).

[19] Originally published in *Epoch,* "The Hunted" was the first-prize
winner in the 1951 *Prize Stories,* ed. Herschel Brickell (New York:
Doubleday, 1951).

[20] George Garrett, "The Old Army Game," *Cold Ground Was My Bed
Last Night* (Columbia: Univ. of Missouri Press, 1964).

as an interpreter with the American Army after the German Occupation of Italy, the second a panoramic novella about a Hungarian war photographer eventually killed in Java, particularly effective in its reminiscences of London during the bombings;[21] Ivan Gold's (1932–) "The Nickel Misery of George Washington Carver Brown" and "Taub East," the first a sardonic version of the basic-training theme, the second a novella centering around the experiences of a schizoid rabbinical student from the Bronx with the Occupation Forces in Japan;[22] James Jones's (1921–) *The Pistol*, a fine novella centering around the experiences of an American private in the aftermath of Pearl Harbor;[23] Edward Loomis's (1924–) "Friendship" and "A Marriage," about, successively, a warlover who discovers his reason-for-being in combat and an infantryman from Texas near the end of the war in Europe;[24] Robie Macauley's (1919–) "The Mind Is Its Own Place," one of four good stories concerning the Counter-Intelligence Corps, highlighted by the portrayal of a young captain who is rumored to be the bombardier who dropped the atomic bomb on Nagasaki;[25] Norman Mailer's (1923–) "The Paper House," concerning two American soldiers in Japan after the

[21] "For Better, for Worse" and "Till Death Do Us Part" are included in Martha Gellhorn's *Two by Two* (New York: Simon and Schuster, 1958); several of her stories concerning European exiles uprooted by war and its aftermath are included in *The Honeyed Peace* (New York: Doubleday, 1953).

[22] "The Nickel Misery of George Washington Carver Brown" and "Taub East" are included in Ivan Gold's *Nickel Miseries, A Collection* (New York: Viking, 1963).

[23] James Jones, *The Pistol* (New York: Scribner, 1959).

[24] Both of Loomis's stories and a third war story, "Friendship," are included in his *Heroic Love* (New York: Knopf, 1960).

[25] Robie Macauley, "The Mind Is Its Own Place," *The End of Pity and Other Stories* (New York: McDowell-Obolensky, 1957).

end of the Pacific War, and their women;[26] Philip Roth's
(1933–) "Defender of the Faith," narrated by a Jewish combat non-commissioned officer attempting to train a group of
Jewish recruits—one of them a bad soldier, a bad Jew, and a
bad human being;[27] Vern Sneider's "A Pail of Oysters," about
a Chinese peasant in postwar Formosa, harried by hunger
and the tyranny of China's save-the-country army;[28] and William Styron's (1925–) superb novella, "The Long March,"
perhaps the greatest piece of shorter fiction to come out of
the War.[29]

The best serious short fiction of World War II tends to be
more concerned with the effects of war upon the individuals who in one way or another participated in it than in
the depiction of acts of war in themselves. The war fiction
is extremely varied, touching as it does upon every phase of
the war, from basic training to occupation, and from death
in combat, prisoner of war compound, or concentration camp
to quiet moments of revelation, exaltation, or remorse. It is
characterized by a depth of emotion and a genuine need to
communicate experience; it is often illuminated by recognition of the importance of the individual and belief in his
rights at a time when the individual was almost lost in the
sweep of great events and when life was being destroyed
more rapidly than at any other time in history. Like the officer in Critchell's "Flesh and Blood," many of the charac-

[26] "The Paper House" appeared originally in *New World Writing*
and is included in Fenton's *Best Short Stories of World War II*.
[27] Philip Roth, "Defender of the Faith," *Goodbye, Columbus* (Boston:
Houghton Mifflin, 1959).
[28] Vern Sneider, "A Pail of Oysters," *A Long Way from Home and
Other Stories* (New York: Putnam, 1956).
[29] Originally published in *Discovery*, "The Long March" is included
in Fenton's *Best Short Stories of World War II*.

ters of the war literature become more finely aware of the importance of love and the importance of man in wartime than they ever were in peacetime: "If you hated the war enough, he thought, as he tramped back along the wet road to camp, it made you love people." [30] It is a paradox, an irony, and a cause for hope that out of the meaninglessness of war grew some of the most meaningful fiction of recent years—a fiction often grim, savage, bewildered, but frequently animated by at least the hope for a concept of human beings as far from perfect but not blind puppets in a frantic, meaningless dance of death.[31]

II. *"There Is No Revolutionary Situation in America"**

The militant Marxist literature of the twenties and thirties had just about run its course before the beginnings of World War II.[32] The end of the Depression and the growing disillusionment with Russia hastened its decline; the Soviet-Nazi Pact of 1939 and America's entry into the War marked

[30] Critchell, "Flesh and Blood," p. 58.
[31] Dodson, "The Let-Down," p. 100.
* Robert Wolf, contributing editor of *The New Masses* in a talk at the Communist Academy in Moscow late in 1927 on the eve of what was to prove to be the most revolutionary decade in the history of American literature.
[32] For a good recent history and commentary, see Daniel Aaron, *Writers on the Left; Episodes in American Literary Communism* (New York: Harcourt, Brace & World, 1961).

its demise. In the face of war's wholesale death and destruction, far-reaching social disorganization, and full employment and fat paychecks back home, the Marxist concept of literature as a weapon in the battle between capitalism and the working class had become anachronistic. The "realistic" proletarian story of class conflict or the exploitation of the havenots by the haves or the delineation of specific economic, political, and social injustice faded away like the memories of the Depression. In its place, as we have seen, there arose the war story; escape fiction with little or no connection with reality as such; stories glorifying the American past; stories of science fiction and fantasy; stories centering around such contemporary problems as the breakdown of a marriage and its effect on a misunderstood or unloved child. Most important of all, as the defeat of the Axis became inevitable, and coincident with the emergence of more and more revelations of the Nazi persecution of the Jews, there developed a swelling tide of stories of injustice of all sorts, particularly those concerned with the role of the Jew in postwar America and the postwar world. The fiction concerned with social problems, particularly those problems growing out of racial injustice, was a far cry from the one-dimensional propaganda stories of the thirties. The socially conscious short stories of the forties and fifties possessed artistry as well as significance. They concerned human beings with problems, not just the problems themselves. They were compounded of deep feeling, understanding, and skill. They existed, in short, like all literature worthy of the name, as art, as entertainment, and as idea.

The major achievement of the socially conscious short story of the last twenty years has been that of a varied group of highly talented American Jews concerned primarily with the role of the Jew in contemporary America. As Harold U. Ribalow, the most knowledgeable student and critic of

Jewish-American literature, has commented, the "contemporary Jewish short story is as vital and provocative as any
short fiction now being offered to the American public." [33]
Of this varied literature of short story collections, perhaps the
most distinguished single volume is Bernard Malamud's
(1914–) *The Magic Barrel* (1958). Whatever their settings
—three of the thirteen stories take place in Italy, the re-
mainder in and around New York City—or mood—which
ranges from the comic to the serio-comic or tragic—Malamud's stories are concerned with intimate crises in the lives
of ordinary lower- to middle-class individuals: the shoemaker whose assistant is in love with his daughter of "The
First Seven Years," a story warm with the family affection
which is so much a part of Jewish life and literature, and
compassionate in its portrayal of the worried father who
dreams of a better life for his daughter than he had had, to at-
tain which he had "slaved and destroyed his heart with anxiety and labor";[34] the aged Jew of "The Mourners," who is
evicted from his tenement room but keeps returning to the
only place in which he feels he belongs, until both he and
the landlord are half mad, a story permeated by a profound
and haunting melancholy which is at once realistic and alive
with the "accents of the hallucinated, the visionary, and the
bizarre";[35] a Columbia University graduate student and his
frantic efforts to obtain an apartment in Rome;[36] a young,

[33] Harold U. Ribalow, Introduction, *The Chosen* (London, New York:
Abelard-Schuman, 1959), p. 9. Mr. Ribalow's other anthologies of
Jewish-American short stories are similarly valuable: *This Land, These
People* (1950) and *These Your Children* (1954); his *Treasury of
American Jewish Stories* (1958) contains essentially the same stories,
along with an excellent introduction.
[34] Bernard Malamud, "The First Seven Years," *The Magic Barrel*
(New York: Farrar, Straus & Cudahy, 1958), p. 15.
[35] *The Magic Barrel*, Alfred Kazin quoted on the dust jacket.
[36] "Behold the Key."

obscure novelist for "whom nothing comes easy";[37] and the fantastic New York rabinnical student and the fish-eating marriage broker of the title story.

Malamud's people are brilliantly individualized; his gift for characterization is often breathtaking. At the same time, however, his characters are Jews in the generic sense. The reader is constantly aware of the almost palpable presence of persecution and misunderstanding which is as much a part of Malamud's characters as the flesh of their bodies, and has made them bellicose, thick-skinned, or painfully vulnerable, a presence almost as old as history yet as recent as Buchenwald.

Man or woman, young or old, intellectual or shopkeeper, Malamud's characters are hagridden by a sense of injustice and grief. All of them, one way or another, live with the awareness of past persecutions, just as truly and painfully as does Isabella, the young woman of "The Lady of the Lake" who has "tatooed [sic] on . . . [her] soft and tender flesh a bluish line of distorted numbers," [38] the stigmata of the concentration camp where she had been interned as a child. " 'I can't marry you,' " Isabella tells the young American Jew in disguise who has gone to Europe in search of romance. " 'I can't marry you. We are Jews. My past is meaningful to me. I treasure what I suffered for.' " [39]

This atavistic identification with past grief is as much a part of Malamud's stories as his marvelous language (he captures what seems to be the essence of American Yiddish, primarily by syntax), his robust humor, his striking and vivid contrasts, and his seemingly complete understanding of his characters and their ways of life. At once grotesque

[37] "The Girl of My Dreams."
[38] "The Lady of the Lake," p. 132.
[39] *Ibid.*

and curiously noble, often ridiculous but endowed with courage and the ability to endure (not silently; far from it!), Malamud's people stand up and face the onslaughts of the world as often as they retreat from them. Malamud's depiction of their struggles, defeats, and small triumphs is completely individualistic, but never freakish or exhibitionistic.[40]

Among the younger Jewish writers, Philip Roth seems the most talented, the most ambitious, the most worth listening to. His first book, a novella and five stories, *Goodbye, Columbus* (1959), won the National Book Award for fiction, as had Malamud's *Magic Barrel;* a subsequent novel indicated that Roth was no one-book sensation, but an author to be reckoned with over what looks to be an important long haul. Like Malamud, Roth knows his people well, and depicts them with humor, compassion, irony, affection, impatience, and occasional dislike. Like Malamud he is deeply concerned with family, societal, and individual relation-

[40] Some of these comments originally appeared in my "Dogged by a Sense of Injustice and Grief," *New York Times Book Review* (May 11, 1958). Malamud's second collection, *Idiots First* (New York: Farrar, Straus, 1963), appeared after this study was completed. With the exception of "A Choice of Profession," these eleven stories and a scene from a play concern characters and situations similar to those of *The Magic Barrel.* Arthur Fidelman, the central character of Malamud's earlier "The Last Mohican," resumes his art studies in Italy in two of the stories, while most of the others are set in or around metropolitan New York, and concern lower- to middle-class American Jews—shopkeepers, pawnbrokers, rabbis, tenement-dwellers—hovering upon the brink of disaster, and, more often than not, tumbling into the abyss. The stories range in tone from the comedy, absurdity, and pathos of the Fidelman pieces to the savagery of "The Jewbird," or the memorable blending of destruction and possible salvation of the title story; they are moving, compassionate, grotesque, and disturbing by turns.

ships. Like Malamud he can transmute ordinary experiences and insignificant characters into something both familiar and strange, something that has about it the occasional fey, mad, hallucinated touch so characteristic of Yiddish and Jewish fiction.

Neil Klugman, the protagonist of Roth's title novella, is characteristic of many of Roth's young Jews. A thoroughly mixed-up youth in an equally mixed-up society, he is vacillating, pompous, and often irritating. He is tormented by feelings both of inferiority and superiority, and he is ruthlessly honest, in his fashion, and admirable in his efforts to find some kind of meaning and some measure of self-realization—and self-justification—in his segment of society, a world troubled by memories of a frequently shabby past which are in conflict with an uncertain present. Neil's summer affair with Brenda Patimkin and her new-rich family (country club out of Newark by Patimkin's Kitchen and Bathroom Sinks) is an effective mingling of conventional boy-pursues-girl and portrait of the artist as a youth materials, occasionally narrated with a fondness for clinical detail reminiscent of "The Princess with the Golden Hair." The two worlds—Neil's and the Patimkins'—are very vividly brought to life, and Neil's inner struggle is perceptively delineated: "What was it inside me that had turned pursuit and clutching into love, and then turned it inside out again? What was it that had turned winning into losing, and losing—who knows —into winning?" [41]

Most of Roth's major characters are similarly adrift in a limbo between past and future, and beset with problems involving their own identities or their places and roles in a changing society. He writes with equal skill and awareness of a pre-adolescent boy who rushes to the top of a building and threatens to kill himself unless his dominating mother

[41] Philip Roth, "Goodbye, Columbus," *Goodbye, Columbus,* p. 135.

and the family rabbi reject the story of the Virgin Birth ("The Conversion of the Jews"), of a young lawyer on the edge of emotional collapse when his suburban security is threatened ("Eli the Fanatic"), of an elder Leopold Bloom type whose domestic troubles include a daughter turned Socialist who is having an affair with a folksinger, his wife's loss of beauty, a love affair with complications, *and* a heart attack ("Epstein"), and a group of wartime Jews in Missouri, his only story not set in or around metropolitan or suburban New York or New Jersey ("Defender of the Faith").[42]

Whereas Malamud and Roth and the other leading American-born Jewish fiction writers are alike in their preoccupation with the American Jew in contemporary society, Isaac Bashevis Singer (1904–) is essentially concerned with echoes of a Jewish past extending to pre-historic days where "time stands still . . . Adam remains naked, Eve lustful . . . Cain kills Abel, the flea lies with the elephant, the flood falls from heaven, the Jews knead clay in Egypt, Job scratches at his sore-covered body." [43] *Gimpel the Fool* (1957), and *The Spinoza of Market Street* (1961), are unique in recent fiction. Singer, born, in Radzymin, Poland, and since 1935 an American resident, is unquestionably one of the major fiction writers of this generation.

Singer's stories are an unforgettable blending of striking contrasts—the old and the new, realism and fantasy, order and change, the ordinary and the spectral. They are compounded of a wild humor, unearthiness, and verisimilitude as convincing as a Baedeker; they are constantly preoccu-

[42] Some of these comments originally appeared in my "In A Limbo Between Past and Present," *New York Times Book Review* (May 17, 1959).
[43] I. B. Singer, "The Mirror," *Gimpel the Fool and Other Stories* (New York: Noonday, 1957), p. 85.

pied with the gulf and the bridge between illusion and reality—"No doubt the world is entirely an imaginary world, but it is only once removed from the true world." [44] Individually impressive, in toto they constitute a panorama of Jewish folklore, tradition, myth, and life which on the one hand is haunted by the past, by the occult, spectral, and demonic, and on the other is alive with the sights and sounds of the Polish ghettoes of the late nineteenth and twentieth centuries.

Among Singer's basically realistic stories are "The Spinoza of Market Street," with its unforgettable portrayal of Dr. Nahum Fishelson, a Warsaw philosopher, and his marriage to the derelict food vendor, Black Dobbe, and consequent redemption as a human being, a vivid depiction of the contrast between the scientific, completely rational life and the emotional, personal urges of man; "Caricature," another story of an elderly Warsaw philosopher and his wife during Hitler's rise to power; "Gimpel the Fool," the individualistic story of the baker of Frampol and his whoreish wife; and "The Little Shoemaker," the family saga of Abba Shuster, the best shoemaker in Frampol.

At the other extreme are stories like "The Black Wedding," "A Tale of Two Liars," "The Destruction of Kreshev," and "The Mirror," which range from the ghettoes of Warsaw or the village of Krashnik to a region inhabited by incubi and succubi, imps, demons, and the Devil himself. These stories of wild and vivid contrast are vibrant with the high, singing poetry of the supernatural and the hallucinated, piercing in their portrayal of crime and punishment, sin and redemption, and universal in their implications.[45]

[44] "Gimpel the Fool," *Gimpel the Fool and Other Stories*, p. 21.
[45] "The Spinoza of Market Street," "Caricature," "The Black Wedding," "A Tale of Two Liars," and "The Destruction of Kreshev" are

Singer's strange world of contrasts and opposites simply *is*.[46] It is real and convincing in the same way that Rousseau's jungle paintings or Chagall's *Arabische Nächte* illustrations are real and convincing. In each case, the creator's vision is so complete, so whole, so harmonious within its own juxta-position of opposites, that only the irremediably literally minded individual questions the appearance of Yadwigha's comfortable bourgeois red sofa in the middle of a leafy jun-gle, or rejects Chagall's bemused and beautiful gold, pink, blue, and emerald-fleshed women, or bizarre, aworldly animals, birds, and fish. Similarly the hallucinated bride-to-be of Singer's "The Black Wedding." Hindele *knows* that the "fancy garments" of her attendants "hid heads grown with elf-locks, goose-feet, unhuman navels, long snouts. The sashes of the young men were snakes in reality, their sable hats were actually hedgehogs, their beards clusters of worms. The men spoke Yiddish and sang familiar songs, but the noise they made was really the bellowing of oxen, the hiss-ing of vipers, the howling of wolves. The musicians had tails, and horns grew from their heads. The maids who at-tended Hindele had canine paws, hoofs of calves, snouts of pigs. The wedding jester was all beard and tongue. The . . . relatives . . . were lions, bears, boars. . . . Alas,

---

in *The Spinoza of Market Street* (New York: Farrar, Straus & Cudahy, 1961); the other stories cited are from *Gimpel the Fool*.

[46] Contrast is, in effect, the key to Singer's esthetic. Satan's comments on the depraved Schloimele are an effective summation of the matter: "Those who understand the complexities of human nature know that joy and pain, ugliness and beauty, love and hate, mercy and cruelty and other conflicting emotions often blend and cannot be separated from each other. Thus I am able not only to make people turn away from the Creator, but to damage their own bodies, all in the name of some imaginary cause." ("The Destruction of Kreshev," p. 198.)

this was not a human wedding, but a Black Wedding." [47]

There are many other important collections of stories by and about American Jews. Among them are Charles Angoff's (1902–) *When I Was a Boy in Boston* (1947), and *Something of My Father and Other People* (1956), sketches, stories, and vignettes concerning an immigrant Jewish family in early twentieth-century Boston and depicting various phases and changes in Jewish life in America from childhood to old age.

Burton Bernstein's (1932–) *The Grove* (1961) is a sequence of essentially amiable, unpretentious, sometimes trivial stories and narrative sketches concerning the summer colony experiences of a small group of highly articulate middle-class Jewish families at "The Grove," a modest resort on the shores of Lake Massasoit, twenty-five miles from Boston.

Harold Brodkey's previously discussed *First Love and Other Sorrows* (1957), are warmhearted and deftly written stories of the St. Louis boyhood of a protagonist only mildly disturbed by his Jewishness, and subsequent events in the lives of somewhat older similar characters, as college students and young husbands and fathers. [48]

Leslie Fiedler's (1917–) *Pull Down Vanity* (1962) contains angry and often pitiless depictions of middle-class emptiness and decadence, characterized by the author's instinctive flair for the depiction of vulgarity and what seems to be an almost compulsive fondling of the hoofs, hide, entrails, and excrement of naturalistic detail.

Herbert Gold's (1924–) *Love and Like* (1960) are varied

---

[47] "The Black Wedding," pp. 30–31.

[48] "Being Jewish also disturbed me, because it meant I could never be one of the golden people—the blond athletes, with their easy charm. If my family had been well off, I might have felt otherwise, but I doubt it." (Harold Brodkey, "The State of Grace," *First Love and Other Sorrows* [New York: Dial, 1957], p. 18.)

and for the most part impressive stories including "Encounter in Haiti" with its memorable characterization of a French fascist in Haiti.[49] Other notable stories in the collection are the family reminiscences of the son of a Jewish grocer, "The Heart of the Artichoke," and "Susanna at the Beach," about a young girl who almost loses her suit at a Cleveland bathing beach, evoking varied reactions in the spectators, and the effective title story.

Ivan Gold's previously mentioned *Nickel Miseries* (1963) concerns characters—white, yellow, or black; Americans, Europeans, and Japanese—who are outsiders of one sort or other whose confrontation with institutional, societal, or individual prejudice furnish subject and theme for all five stories and novellas.[50]

James Jaffe's *Poor Cousin Evelyn* (1951) are competent stories of well-to-do Jewish life in New York as are Arthur Kober's (1900–) many deft and humorous dialect sketches and stories about life in the Bronx, particularly as lived by Pa and Ma Gross and their daughter Bella whose continuing efforts to meet the right marriageable man are the backbone of *Thunder Over the Bronx* (1935), *My Dear Bella* (1941), and *Bella, Bella, Kissed A Fella* (1951).[51]

---

[49] Originally published in *Midstream,* "Encounter in Haiti" was the second-prize winner in the 1957 *Prize Stories,* ed. Paul Engle (New York: Doubleday, 1957).

[50] "Taub East" and "The Nickel Misery of George Washington Carver Brown" are particularly notable. The first centers around a one-time rabbinical student from the Bronx stationed at an American Army base in Japan; Taub is morbidly sensitive because he's convinced that the Asiatics are increasingly anti-Semitic, and precipitates a series of incidents which culminate in tragedy; "Nickel Misery" concerns an inept Negro recruit's experiences with various kinds of intolerance—white and Negro—during basic training in Georgia.

[51] Kober is also the author of three other collections similar in mood and method to the Bella stories: *Pardon Me for Pointing* (1939), *That*

Grace Paley's *The Little Disturbances of Man* (1959)
center for the most part around Jewish women in and around
New York City, and are characterized by a briskly individualistic method and sharply comic vision.

Leonard Q. Ross's (Leo Rosten, 1908–) *The Education of
H*Y*M*A*N Kaplan* (1939) and *The Return of H*Y*-
M*A*N K*A*P*L*A*N* (1959), about the ebullient Mr.
Kaplan's night school activities, constitute a refreshing contrast to the customary more somber or sober treatment of
such characters, although Ross has sometimes been criticized by authorities on Jewish literature for indulging in
caricature.

J. D. Salinger's talented and highly articulate Glass family
has been previously commented on; the Glasses appear in
Nine Stories (1953), *Franny and Zooey* (1961), and *Raise
High the Roof Beam, Carpenters and Seymour—an Introduction* (1963), with promises of more installments to come.

Delmore Schwartz's (1913–) *The World Is a Wedding*
(1948) and *Successful Love* (1961) are well-intentioned
but uneven. Schwartz is at his best in relatively brief, realistic stories like "The Gift" which concern nothing more momentous than a child's experiences in subway and taxi from
Manhattan to Brooklyn. A fantasy like "The Track Meet" is
an unsuccessful fusing of the real and the surreal or illusory,
and pieces like "An American Fairy Tale" are essentially essays rather than stories.[52]

Many of Irwin Shaw's best known stories, some of them

Man Is Here Again (1946), and *Ooh, What You Said* (1958), all
published by Simon & Schuster.
[52] All of the stories cited are from Schwartz's second collection of
stories, *Successful Love and Other Stories*, (New York: Corinth,
1961).

previously discussed, concern the role of the Jew in America and in the world; "Act of Faith" and "Sailor Off the Bremen" are probably his best-known and most frequently anthologized stories. Lesser-known pieces include "God on Friday Night," an effective if oversimplified contrast between a Yiddish mother and her nightclub entertainer son; "Medal from Jerusalem," an extremely moving if contrived wartime story of an American army officer and a Jewish girl highlighted by the character of an Arab journalist with a consuming hatred of the Jews;[53] "The Passion of Lance Corporal Hawkins," centering around the arrival of a shipload of Jews in Palestine and the effects of this incident upon a varied group of Jew-haters; and "The Man with One Arm," an involved hugger-mugger of espionage, counter-espionage, and anti-Semitism in Occupied Berlin.

Jerome Weidman's (1913–) selected stories, *My Father Sits in the Dark* (1961), contain many stories of lower- and middle-class Jewish life in New York City. Weidman is thoughtful, entertaining, and a skillful professional, but his stories are more often competent reportage, like "Gallantry in Action," one of the most effective depictions of non-violent anti-Semitism of recent years, than distinguished fiction. It can be said that this prolific author seldom if ever wrote a bad story, but, on the other hand, never wrote one really as good as his talent and seriousness of purpose might lead one to expect.

Samuel Yellen (1906–), on the other hand, in *The Passionate Shepherd* (1957), has written two of the best Jewish stories in recent years: "Your Children Will Burn," about a big operator, James Moss, née Jacob Mosskovitz, a Middle

---

[53] "I have nothing against the Jews . . . but I will fight to the death to keep even one more Jew from entering the country" ("Medal from Jerusalem," *Mixed Company,* p. 338).

Western junk dealer; and "The Four Sides of a Triangle," an adolescent's account of Jewish family life, again in the Midwest.

Eugene Ziller's *In This World* (1960) concerns second-generation shopkeepers, garment workers, tenement- or apartment-dwellers, and occasional professional men in and around New York City; particularly effective are the title story, with its contrast between the older and the younger generation, and "My Father and the Cossacks."

Although the number of stories concerning the American Negro increased greatly during the war years and thereafter, there is as yet no body of recent short fiction by and about American Negroes which is comparable in variety, extent, and achievement to the Jewish-American short stories just discussed. Richard Wright's (1908–1960) *Eight Men* (1961) contains some savagely memorable scenes, but Wright's characters—misunderstood, exploited, or vilely misused by white villains—tend to be as one-dimensional as the run-of-the-mill stereotypes of the proletarian literature of the thirties. As a sad and often moving testimonial to the result of racial intolerance on a gifted and bitterly disillusioned human being, *Eight Men* is memorable and disturbing, but as a creative work it is second rate.

The "Simple" sketches of Langston Hughes (1902–), along with *Laughing to Keep from Crying* (1952), seem to me the best recent collections of stories about Negroes by a Negro, if these unpretentious "Simple" pieces about Negro life in Harlem can be classified as fiction.[54] Many of the *Laughing*

---

[54] Selections from *Simple Speaks His Mind* (1950), *Simple Takes a Wife* (1952), and *Simple Stakes A Claim* (1957), are included in *The Langston Hughes Reader* (New York: Braziller, 1958), along with four stories from his early (1934) short story collection, *The Ways of*

to Keep from Crying pieces are similarly a combination of narrative, autobiography, reminiscence, and essay. Deftly and often humorously narrated, but serious and occasionally understandably bitter beneath the surfaces, a story such as "Who's Passing for Who?" is Hughes at his best. Colloquial, relaxed, and anecdotal in method, this story of two very different kinds of Harlem intellectuals and three visiting schoolteachers from Iowa suggests more about the essential nature of intolerance and atavistic reactions to Negro-white relations than most of Wright's savage denunciations.

The number of really good recent stories by and about American Negroes is similarly limited. One thinks of Frank Yerby's (1916–) first published story, "Health Card," a moving if somewhat unconvincing depiction of the humiliation suffered by a Negro soldier and his wife at a Southern army camp;[55] James Baldwin's (1924–) "Sonny's Blues" and "This Morning, This Evening, So Soon";[56] Ann Petry's (1911–) "Miss Muriel," or Paule Marshall's (1929–) "Brooklyn";[57] and

---

White Folks, and eight stories from *Laughing to Keep from Crying*, including "Who's Passing for Who?" *The Reader* also contains poems, plays, articles, and speeches, and selections from Hughes's autobiography and miscellaneous writings.

[55] "Health Card" was originally published in *Harper's* and was anthologized in the 1944 *Prize Stories*, ed. Herschel Brickell (New York: Doubleday, Doran, 1944), where it received the award for the best "first" story of the year.

[56] "Sonny's Blues" and "This Morning, This Evening, So Soon" first appeared in *Partisan Review* and the *Atlantic*, respectively, and are included in the *Best American Short Stories* of 1958 and 1961, ed. Martha Foley and David Burnett (Boston: Houghton Mifflin, 1958, 1961).

[57] Ann Petry's novella "Miss Muriel" originally appeared in *Soon, One Morning: New Writing by American Negroes, 1940–1962*, ed. Herbert Hill (New York: Knopf, 1963); it is part of a longer work

after this it becomes difficult to single out stories which have survived the changes in the social and ethical climate in which they were produced.[58] This scarcity of good Negro stories can perhaps be explained by the very gravity of the Negro situation in America during the postwar years, a seriousness which renders impossible the objectivity and maturity of thought vitally necessary for the creation of literature as opposed to social commentary in fictional form.[59]

The development of a minority literature, particularly that of a persecuted minority, seems almost inevitably to follow a similar pattern. Much modern Hebrew fiction, for example, as Joel Blocker and Robert Alter have pointed out in

---

of fiction currently in progress. Paule Marshall's "Brooklyn" is in her *Soul Clap Hands and Sing* (New York: Atheneum, 1961).

[58] With the exceptions already noted, it seems to me that the best portrayals of Negroes in short fiction since 1940 have been by white Southerners, notably Faulkner, Eudora Welty, Flannery O'Connor, Peter Taylor, Ellen Douglas, and others. For the most part, however, stories about Negroes by white authors, particularly non-Southerners, including some anthologized in both the *Best* and *Prize* annual collections of "distinguished" American short stories, have been embarrassingly bad—sentimentalized, oversimplified, vulgarized, often based on little understanding of either Negroes or whites, and for the most apparently written either out of misguided good intentions or to exploit a current situation.

[59] On the other hand, the period has produced some very good novels, from Ralph Ellison's *Invisible Man* (1952) to John A. Williams's *Sissie* (1963). Very few Negro short stories compare with these and several other novels in depth and artistry. Characteristically, most of the fiction section of *Soon, One Morning* consists of excerpts from novels rather than short stories, and, except for Ann Petry's "Miss Muriel" and Cyrus Colter's "The Beach Umbrella," these excerpts are considerably more impressive than the short stories. Herbert Hill's introduction to *Soon, One Morning* is a good survey and commentary on recent Negro writing in America.

an excellent recent collection of Israeli stories, is still essentially didactic;[60] it is a truism that the older generation of Hebrew fiction writers has been more concerned with what it means to be a Jew than with what it means to be a human being, more preoccupied with the Hebrew situation than with the human situation. On the other hand, the younger generation of Israeli writers, including those who possess the deepest commitment to basic Zionist beliefs, are both polemicists and artists, Zionists and citizens of the world. Similarly, the American Jew has passed from the period of acute consciousness of his Jewishness to an awareness of his position as a Jewish American. Like Malamud and Roth, both of whom constantly remind us that the Jew *is* different[61] and that his role in America is often difficult and uncertain —still compounded of bewilderment and hostility and pride —most of the best recent Jewish-American fiction writers, as Harold Ribalow has commented, are less neurotic about their Jewishness than their predecessors, and are more and more likely to write out of knowledge rather than ignorance of Jewish-Gentile relations in America, more likely to write with compassion than bitterness, and to create with awareness that their fiction will aid, partially, in creating the portrait of the American Jew which the Gentile will see and judge—in short that they are Jewish-Americans rather than Jews-in-America.[62]

Similarly, it seems to me, the Negro-American writer. Not until the violent emotions engendered by the racial crisis in

[60] Joel Blocker, Preface, and Robert Alter, Introduction, *Israeli Stories; A Selection of the Best Contemporary Hebrew Writing* (New York: Schocken, 1962).

[61] Sheldon Grossbart in Philip Roth's "Defender of the Faith" is characteristic: " 'Because I'm a Jew . . . I *am* different. Better, maybe not. But different.' " (*Goodbye, Columbus*, p. 188.)

[62] Harold U. Ribalow, Introduction, *The Chosen*, p. 10.

America subside will there exist in America a climate hospitable for the creation of a Negro-American literature comparable to the Jewish-American fiction of the past decade or two. Only when the contemporary American climate makes it possible for a writer to think of himself as a Negro-American rather than a Negro-in-America will it be possible for him, as Herbert Hill has observed, to "break through the limits of racial parochialism into the whole range of the modern writer's preoccupations." [63] And if this occurs, the production of a vital Negro-American literature is likely to be one of the major directions the short fiction of the next decade will take.

III. *"The Woods Are Full of Regional Writers"*

Except for Poe's stories, which usually take place in a nebulous never-never region "out of Space" and "out of Time," the American short story has tended to be firmly rooted in specific locales or settings, whether such backgrounds are just a stage where the action of the story occurs or whether they imply the realistic preoccupation with locality of the mid–twentieth century regionalists or involve a concept of place as a pervasive moral-sociological-cultural-historical-economic reality.

Commenting on the virtual disappearance of dialect in the American short story, Edward Weeks has suggested that the reason for this disappearance is an increasing nationalism and the comparative absence of marked differences among

[63] Herbert Hill, Introduction, *Soon, One Morning*, p. 3.

Americans.[64] Recent newspaper headlines from Tuscaloosa
or Chicago, Oxford, or Washington, D.C., tend to weaken
the validity of his speculations, but Mr. Weeks's comments
about dialect are valid and could be extended to include
most of the trappings of the old-fashioned local color or regional story. Today, a century after Bret Harte's gamblers-
with-integrity and prostitutes-with-hearts-of-gold began
what was to become a craze for the local color, dialect story,[65]
regionalism has almost become a dirty word usually equated
with mediocrity, limited parochialism, shallowness, folksi-
ness, and artificiality. "In the South," as Flannery O'Connor
has commented, "there are more amateur writers than there
are rivers and streams. In almost every hamlet you'll find at
least one lady writing epics in Negro dialect and probably
two or three old gentlemen who have impossible historical
novels on the way. The woods are full of regional writers,
and it is the great horror of every serious Southern writer
that he will become one of them." [66]

The serious recent fiction writer has increasingly tended
to avoid the detailed photographic realism of his immediate
predecessors, and to shun the tricks and affectations of the

---

[64] Edward Weeks: "Contemporary American and Russian Writers:
Trends and Forces," Summer Session lecture, University of Colorado,
July 24, 1961.

[65] For a good survey of the history and development of the local color
story, see Harry R. Warfel's and G. Harrison Orians's Introduction to
American Local-Color Stories (New York: American, 1941), pp. ix–
xxiv.

[66] Flannery O'Connor, "The Fiction Writer and His Country," pp. 159–
160. Similarly, Eudora Welty: " 'Regional,' I think, is a careless term,
as well as a condescending one, because what it does is fail to differ-
entiate between the localized raw material of life and its outcome as
art. 'Regional' is an outsider's term; it has no meaning for the insider
who is doing the writing." ("Place in Fiction," *South Atlantic Quarterly* [Jan. 1956], p. 72.)

run-of-the-mill local color story of the past with its one-dimensional actors and its hand-tinted settings labeled Missouri, California, New Hampshire, *et al.* He is not over-concerned with the external depiction of landscape, or with local custom, dialect, and dress for their own sakes. He is concerned with an attempt to glimpse that which is universal in the specific, that which is archetypal in the individual, whether that individual is presented in Saroyan's California vineyards, Eudora Welty's Mississippi, James T. Farrell's Chicago, Bernard Malamud's New York City, H. L. Davis's Oregon, or Donald Windham's Georgia.

In this sense regionalism, or what can more properly be called the "sense of place," is not mere embroidery or decoration to be added to a short story as one hangs ornaments on a Christmas tree or pastes brightly colored stickers on a gift package. In this sense, it is a basic and indispensable element of fiction, a kind of fifth dimension, as important as or in some cases more important than character, situation, plot, or idea. It is both a seminal force and a unifying principle which can shape a work of fiction, and give the fullest extent of meaning and drama and vitality to the characters and events within it; it can be something, as Eudora Welty has observed, upon which "fiction depends for its life . . . as essential to good and honest writings as a logical mind." [67]

The New South is the region which has produced the most likely to endure recent body of short fiction in America, stories so varied and individualistic as to reject academic labels such as a "Southern school" of writers, and so universal in their implications as to repudiate the appellation of "distinctly regional" literature. The reasons underlying the Southern literary renaissance have been widely analyzed, com-

[67] Eudora Welty, "Place in Fiction," pp. 59, 67.

mented on, and theorized about; whatever they may really be, it is not happenstance that many of the most significant fiction writers whose work is inseparably linked with their "country" are Southerners.[68] Nor is it coincidence alone that the work of the greatest American short story writer since Sherwood Anderson, William Faulkner, is as securely rooted in place—and at the same time as universal—as are the stories of one of the greatest of nineteenth-century "regionalists," Nathaniel Hawthorne.[69]

[68] This renaissance has been attributed to a sense of guilt because of the institution of slavery, to a sense of outrage because of the indignities forced upon the South during the Occupation and Reconstruction era, to the glorification of the Lost Cause and the way of life which died with it, to the conflicts between an agrarian and a commercialized society, and the attendant influx of an alien working class, to a heightened awareness of disintegration and death, both individual and societal, and the resultant compulsive search for identity and self-justification in a world whose loyalties, values, and patterns of conduct had been suddenly obliterated. A good summary of these and other factors is in Richmond Croom Beatty, Floyd C. Watkins, and Thomas Daniel Young, "The Southern Renaissance in Letters," *The Literature of the South* (New York: Scott, Foresman, 1952), pp. 611–31. A good selection of essays concerning the social and literary manifestations of the period is in *Southern Renascence: The Literature of the Modern South*, ed. Louis D. Rubin and Robert D. Jacobs (Baltimore: The Johns Hopkins Press, 1953). See also John M. Bradbury, *Renaissance in the South; A Critical History of the Literature, 1920–1960* (Chapel Hill: Univ. of North Carolina Press, 1963).

[69] Though Faulkner never abandoned the short story and wrote some of his best stories after 1940, his major contribution to the field antedates the time limits of this study. The voluminous critical and interpretative literature about Faulkner is primarily concerned with his novels rather than the short stories. A good bibliography is in *William Faulkner: Three Decades of Criticism*, ed. Frederick J. Hoffman and Olga W. Vickery (East Lansing: Michigan State Univ. Press, 1960, reissued by Harcourt, Brace & World, 1963); a less detailed but similarly convenient and helpful bibliography is in Lawrance Thompson,

Like Faulkner's short fiction, the stories of Eudora Welty (1909–) are now recognized as a permanent contribution to the literature of the American short story. *A Curtain of Green* (1941), *The Wide Net* (1943), *The Golden Apples* (1949), and *The Bride of the Innisfallen* (1955) are the works of a rare and original talent and display an individualistic mastery of form and rare understanding of subject. Mississippi, Miss Welty's native state, has furnished subject matter for all of her fiction, with the exception of her most

---

William Faulkner: An Introduction and Interpretation (New York: Barnes & Noble, 1963).

Similarly Katherine Anne Porter (1890–), John Steinbeck (1902–), and Erskine Caldwell (1903–) belong essentially to the period prior to that discussed here, although all of them have continued to write short stories, including Miss Porter's *The Leaning Tower and Other Stories* (New York: Harcourt, Brace), published in 1944 although most of its contents were written and published individually during the thirties. Like Faulkner's, Miss Porter's short fiction has been discussed in detail by many critics; a good introduction is Harry J. Mooney, *The Fiction and Criticism of Katherine Anne Porter* (rev. ed., Pittsburg: Univ. of Pittsburg Press, 1962). Caldwell's best stories, similarly, are with few exceptions products of the years prior to 1940. The inferior quality of much of Caldwell's later work tends to make one forget the importance of his earlier short stories, the vigor and overall excellence of which are manifest in the recent selection from his some hundred and fifty stories—*Erskine Caldwell's Men and Women*, ed. Carvel Collins (Boston: Little, Brown, 1961). I have not included Steinbeck in this chapter for the same reasons, although *The Pastures of Heaven* (New York: Brewer, Warren & Putnam, 1932) and particularly *The Long Valley* (New York: Viking, 1938) are among the classics of twentieth-century short fiction. Nor have I commented on such outstanding writers as Conrad Aiken, William March, Wilbur Daniel Steele, and William Carlos Williams; although their stories appear in "collected" or "selected" editions during the forties and fifties, the stories themselves, with only occasional exceptions, are from volumes which were originally published earlier. See Appendix A.

recent collection,[70] but her range and variety are remarkable, embracing gentle comedy and grim satire, the grotesque and the ordinary, the technically simple and the elaborately indirect and implicational.

In a perceptive and appreciative introduction to *A Curtain of Green,* Katherine Anne Porter has commented on some of the paradoxes and contrasts of Miss Welty's first stories, contrasts which were to appear and reappear in almost all of her later fiction. Perhaps the most significant of these is the contrast between the simplicity of the author's narrative method and the complexity and ambiguity of her themes and moods. "A Piece of News," one of her best and most frequently anthologized stories, is characteristic. Almost stark in its external simplicity, the story concerns a few moments in the lives of Ruby Fisher and her bootlegger husband Clyde. A simple rural girl, Ruby returns to her cabin at the beginning of the story and reads in a newspaper an account of the shooting of a woman who is also named Ruby Fisher. She is shocked, pleased, eventually excited. She fancies herself dying, bedecked in "a brand-new nightgown, her heart . . . hurting with every beat, many times more than her toughened skin when Clyde slapped at her."[71] When Clyde returns to the cabin she is sensuously attracted to him; she "gently" prepares his meal, standing almost tiptoe on "bare, warm feet," almost like a priestess performing a ritual. The coincidence of the newspaper story and her identification with the other Ruby Fisher have made her more intuitively aware of her own being than she has ever been before; the unromantic facts of her drab life have been

---

[70] Four of the seven stories included in *The Bride of the Innisfallen* take place outside of Mississippi.

[71] Eudora Welty, "A Piece of News," *A Curtain of Green and Other Stories* (New York: Harcourt, Brace, 1941), p. 26.

imperceptibly changed and Ruby at the conclusion of the story is not quite the same as Ruby at the beginning, and whether she will ever be quite the same is doubtful.[72]

Beneath the surface simplicity of such a story, Miss Welty probes the enigma of human personality, and suggests the depths of individual identity. Human "relationship," Miss Welty once commented, "*is* a pervading and changing mystery."[73] Her short stories, early and late, are fictional explorations into the nature of this mystery. They possess in common, as Ruth M. Vande Kieft has commented, a preoccupation with the inner life of her characters. They are concerned with basic and universal verities—love and loneliness, joy and sorrow, life and death. If they are alive with a primal loneliness, they also reflect a primal joy. If the private quest for the identity of self which is a common chord in many of her stories ends in defeat as often as victory, Miss Welty's concern with resignation, loneliness, and isolation is more "right'" than tragic.[74]

The most undervalued good Southern short story writer I know of is the late John Bell Clayton (1906–1955) whose posthumous *The Strangers Were There* (1957) deserves to be widely read. Though he lived in California following his retirement from the Charlottesville *Progress* in 1946, Clayton's stories are as Virginian as Joyce's are Irish. They are as deeply rooted in place as Joyce's; they are as universal as Joyce's in their implication. All of them have a common setting, the small city of "Colonial Springs" and its surround-

[72] Some of these comments originally appeared in my "Eudora Welty," *29 Stories* (Boston: Houghton Mifflin, 1960), pp. 336–37.
[73] Eudora Welty, "How I Write," *Virginia Quarterly Review* (Spring 1955), p. 250.
[74] Ruth M. Vande Kieft, *Eudora Welty* (New York: Twayne, United States Authors Series, 1962).

ing country, which is very closely patterned after Charlottesville and Albemarle County where Clayton attended the
University of Virginia and lived most of his life. The place
and its people are keenly observed: the white-columned
mansions of the Yankee millionaires; the foul-smelling back
streets of the paregoric drinkers and the red-lipped girls from
the wrong side of the tracks; the courthouse square with its
heroic statue of General Lee; the Negro district, "Jug Hill,"
exploding into manic activity every Saturday night; the hills
and the hollows of the hunters and the mountain men who
are awkward and ill at ease in town but in their blue hills and
walking softly with dog and gun have about them an inef-
faceable dignity and strength. Clayton was passionately interested in people, as all writers worthy of the name must be
—the unsung but not insignificant little people who are
everywhere and who are the heart and soul of a region or a
way of life: people like gentle Uncle Gene McCantland who
kills the intruder who had murdered his dog, or the violent
Gatemyers and Lowhatters and their feudin', or Antietam
Blankenship who looked like a bird and had his moment of
greatness the day the highway froze over in Cherry Glen.

The narrator of several of these stories, a newspaperman
in Colonial Springs, prays for "that most improbable of all
miracles: that I be permitted to see clearly." [75] John Bell
Clayton did learn to see things clearly, to see them steadily
and see them whole, and to record them with sensitivity and
insight, humor and compassion, affection and indignation.
"It is my native land and I love it," the journalist-narrator
reflects after being witness to the slaying of two Negroes by
a sheriff's deputy, "but there are times when I hate it." [76]

Several of the most important recent Southern short

[75] John Bell Clayton, "An Empty Sunday, the Snow, and the Strangers," *The Strangers Were There* (New York: Macmillan, 1957), p. 12.
[76] "Incident at Chapman's Switch," p. 93. Some of these comments

story writers, including Truman Capote, Carson McCullers, Flannery O'Connor, Peter Taylor, and Tennessee Williams, have been discussed in the preceding chapters. Apart from such writers, some of the most impressive writers of short fiction have come out of the Middle South, among them such disparate authors as Kentucky's Caroline Gordon (1895–) and Jesse Stuart (1907–). Miss Gordon's prose, as Vivienne Koch has observed, is "perhaps the most unaffected and uniformly accomplished that is being written by any American woman today." [77] The best of Miss Gordon's stories, collected in *The Forest of the South* (1946), and with four additional new stories in *Old Red and Other Stories* (1963), have about them the ring of permanence. "The Captive," "The Forest of the South," "The Ice House," "Her Quaint Honor," and others are characterized by intelligence, dignity, and artistry, and are among the very good stories of the period.

Certainly the most prolific short story writer from the region is Jesse Stuart. *Head of W— Hollow* (1936), *Men of the Mountain* (1941), *Tales from the Plum Grove Hills* (1946), *Clearing in the Sky* (1950), and *Plowshare in Heaven* (1958) are written in a fresh, strong voice. Stuart is a good storyteller whose tales move quickly and at their best are vibrantly alive. His humor, sincerity, and affectionate understanding of the Kentucky hill country and its people

---

originally appeared in my "Look at Virginia," *Saturday Review* (June 22, 1957), p. 17. For readers unfamiliar with Clayton's work, the following stories suggest the range of his mood and subject: "The White Circle," "Snowfall on Fourth Street," "The Silence of the Mountains," "The Summer of the Insistent Voices," and "The Man Who Looked Like A Bird."

[77] Vivienne Koch, "The Conservatism of Caroline Gordon," *Southern Renascence*, pp. 325–26.

are a refreshing antidote to the groanings and lamentations of many of the metropolitan Jeremiahs.

So too are Marjorie Kinnan Rawling's (1896–1953) vigorous stories of life among the Florida Crackers, collected in *When the Whippoorwill* (1940), one of the best volumes to come out of the lower Atlantic coastal states. North Carolina has produced more than its share of good story writers; notable collections include the work of older writers like James Boyd's (1888–1944) *Old Pines and Other Stories* (1952), and Paul Green's (1894–) *Salvation on a String* (1946), and *Dog on the Sun* (1949). Other significant volumes include Frances Gray Patton's (1906–) *The Finer Things of Life* (1951), and the work of such talented comparative newcomers as Doris Betts's *The Gentle Insurrection* (1954), and Reynolds Price's (1933–) *The Names and Faces of Heroes.*[78]

Other notable work includes Robert Penn Warren's (1905–) *The Circus in the Attic* (1948); James Still's (1906–1954) *On Troublesome Creek* (1941), which could be claimed by Kentucky which furnishes the settings or by Alabama where the author was born and raised; Thomas Mabry's (1903–) stories of Middle Tennessee's "Black Patch" in *The White Hound* (1960); Tennessee's Andrew Lytle's (1902–) *A Novel, Novella, and Four Stories* (1958); and Ward Dorrance's (1904–) stories of Missouri's Little Dixie in *The White Hound* (1960).[79]

[78] A good selection of North Carolina stories is *North Carolina in the Short Story*, ed. Richard Walser (Chapel Hill: Univ. of North Carolina Press, 1948). The variety of South Carolinian short story writers is similarly indicated in *South Carolina in the Short Story*, ed. Katherine M. Jones and Mary Verner Schlaefer (Columbia: Univ. of South Carolina Press, 1952).

[79] A good representative selection of recent Southern short fiction is *A New Southern Harvest*, ed. Robert Penn Warren and Albert Erskine (New York: Bantam Books, 1957).

Shelby Foote's (1916–) stories and novellas of the Mississippi Delta country, *Jordan Country* (1953), are impressive though occasionally over-melodramatic; so are Walter Clemons's (1929–) Texas stories, *The Poison Tree* (1959). Arkansas's Thyra Samter Winslow (1893–1961) belongs essentially to the period preceding this study, although her last story collection was published in 1954.[80] Shirley Ann Grau's (1929–) subsequent novels have not quite fulfilled the promise of her first book, *The Black Prince* (1954), a memorable collection of stories concerning whites and Negroes in Louisiana. George Garrett's *King of the Mountain* (1957), *In the Briar Patch* (1961), and *Cold Ground Was My Bed Last Night* (1964) contain some first-rate stories of his native Florida. As much Middle South as Southwest are the best stories of three Texas-born authors: Katherine Anne Porter (1890–),[81] William Goyen[82], and William Humphrey (1925–).[83] Oliver La Farge's (1901–) *A Pause in the Desert* (1957) and Fray Angelico Chavez's (1910–) *From An Altar Screen* (1957) represent two quite different kinds of short fiction, each in its way admirable, from New Mexico.[84]

[80] Thyra Winslow's first collection, *Picture Frames*, appeared in 1923; her last, *The Sex Without Sentiment*, was published in 1954.

[81] Miss Porter's most recent story, "Holiday," first-prize winner in the 1962 *Prize Stories* is set in the "deep blackland Texas farm country," not far from the Louisiana border.

[82] Many of the best of Goyen's stories are recollections of Texas, or are set in "Charity," Texas; they include "Old Wildwood," "The Faces of Blood Kindred," "The Armadillo Basket," and "A People of Grass," all from *The Faces of Blood Kindred* (New York: Random House, 1960).

[83] Settings of William Humphrey's *The Last Husband and Other Stories* (New York: Morrow, 1953) range from a Manhattan suburb to the Southwest or Middle South; of the latter, "Quail for Mr. Forester" and "The Shell" are outstanding.

[84] Among the best of La Farge's New Mexico stories are "The Resting Place," "The Happy Indian Laughter," and the title story of *A Pause*

Notable stories from the Far West or the West Coast include Walter VanTilburg Clark's (1909–) *The Watchful
Gods* (1950) and William Saroyan's (1908–) many collections, among them *My Name Is Aram* (1940), *Dear Baby*
(1945), *The Assyrian and Other Stories* (1956). The best of
Clark's stories, like "The Winds and Snows of Winter," are
richly textured and thought-provoking, admirable in their
remarkable evocation of place. Saroyan has been around so
long, and is so prolific, that one tends to forget the importance of his contribution to the American short story; his first
and best-known collection, *The Daring Young Man on the
Flying Trapeze* (1934), brought to the short story a freshness
of vision, simplicity, gaiety, and sympathetic understanding
of little people at a time when the genre was becoming
enmired in an angry social consciousness or basically meaningless slice-of-life realism. In spite of whimsy, repetitive-
ness, and self-imitation, Saroyan's stories are part of the
permanent literature of the American short story, and his
"country"—particularly San Francisco, Fresno, and their
outlying environs—is as real in its way as Faulkner's Mississippi. Particularly effective is Saroyan's depiction of childhood and adolescence; stories like "The Fifty Yard Dash,"
"The Parsley Garden," or "The Home of the Human Race"
and "Winter Vineyard Workers" are little classics which
have about them the warmth of an August afternoon with
the scent of ripening fruit in the air.[85]

---

in the Desert: A Collection of Short Stories (Boston: Houghton Mifflin,
1957). Most of the best stories in La Farge's earlier collection (*All
the Young Men* [Boston: Houghton Mifflin, 1935]) are also concerned
with Indian life in the American Southwest.
[85] "The Fifty Yard Dash" is from *My Name Is Aram* (New York: Harcourt, Brace, 1940); "The Parsley Garden" from *The Assyrian and*

Other good collections out of the West are H. L. Davis's (1896–1960) Oregon stories, *Team Bells Woke Me* (1953), and Vardis Fisher's (1895–) *Love and Death* (1959), including the unforgettable "The Scarecrow" and other Idaho stories which deserve to be better known. A. B. Guthrie's (1901–) *The Big It* (1960) contains deftly written tales, narrative sketches, and stories, some humorous and other serious, re-creating the American West from early in the nineteenth to the middle of our own century. The best stories of Edward Loomis's *Heroic Love* (1960), and Wallace Stegner's (1909–) *The Women on the Wall* (1950) and *The City of the Living* (1956) owe a good deal of their effectiveness to place and setting,[86] and Virginia Sorensen's (1912–) *Where Nothing Is Long Ago* (1963) is a group of memorable stories and personal reminiscences of Mormon life in Utah.

Outstanding collections of distinctly regional short fiction from the Middle West include Mari Sandoz's (1901–) *Hostiles and Friendlies* (1959), although all ten of the stories of rural or small-town Nebraska life included in this collection of autobiography, reminiscence and Nebraska history/legend and folklore were originally written before 1940. So were most of Ruth Suckow's (1892–1960) quietly realistic and

---

Other Stories (New York: Harcourt, Brace, 1950); "The Home of the Human Race" and "The Winter Vineyard Workers" from *The Whole Voyald and Other Stories* (Boston: Little, Brown, 1956).

[86] The title novella and "Mustangs" of Loomis's *Heroic Love* (New York: Knopf, 1960), both excellent stories, are set in or around "Albo," county seat of an eastern California county; the remaining selections are war stories. Eight of *The Women on the Wall* stories (Boston: Houghton Mifflin, 1949) center around incidents in the life of a young boy growing up in Saskatchewan around 1917.

often deeply moving stories of rural and small town life in Iowa, characterized throughout by unpretentious artistry and admirable understanding.[87] Jessamyn West (1907–) has written deftly and sympathetically of an Indiana Quaker community in *The Friendly Persuasion* (1945). Other volumes from the region include Wilbur Schramm's (1907–) *Windwagon Smith and Other Yarns* (1947), tall tales filled with affection for the American frontier past and the fat dark earth of the Iowa farmlands; Iowa's Calvin Kentfield (1925–), now a vociferously first-generation Californian, with *The Angel and the Sailor* (1957) and *The Great Wondering Goony Bird* (1963),[88] and Wisconsin's prolific August Derleth (1909–) with *Sac Prairie People* (1948) and *Wisconsin Earth* (1948).

Nelson Algren (1909–)[89] and James T. Farrell (1904–)

---

[87] Except for *Some Others and Myself* (New York: Rinehart, 1952) Miss Suckow's short fiction belongs to the twenties and thirties: *Iowa Interiors* (New York: Knopf, 1926), *Children and Older People*, (New York: Knopf, 1931), and *Carry-Over* (New York: Farrar & Rinehart, 1936).

[88] The best of Kentfield's first collection, *The Angel and the Sailor; A Novella and Nine Stories* (New York: McGraw-Hill, 1957), including the title piece, center around small town or rural Iowa life near the Mississippi River.

Six of the ten stories in Kentfield's second collection, *The Great Wondering Goony Bird* (New York: Random House, 1963), take place aboard a freighter; of the others, only "Windmills" and "The Rose of Sharon" have a specifically Middle Western setting.

[89] The best and best known of Algren's individualistic stories of first- and second-generation Americans in the jungles of Chicago's west side include "A Bottle of Milk for Mother" and "How the Devil Came Down Division Street." Closely akin to the Leftist literature of the thirties in his sympathy for havenots, rejects, and derelicts, Algren's frequent glorification of such characters is perhaps his most conspicuous shortcoming and brings to mind Katherine Anne Porter's com-

are the outstanding big-city spokesmen from the Middle West.[90] The Chicago of Algren's *Neon Wilderness* (1948) and of Farrell's many collections have become so specifically their *country*, particularly Farrell's, that today it is almost impossible to stop at the corner of Prairie Avenue and Fifty-eighth Street without thinking of Studs Lonigan and his disreputable peers, including the indefatigable Weary Reilly and the dogged Danny O'Neill.

Though there have been some impressive recent stories from and about New England, good collections are scarce. Dorothy Canfield Fisher's (1879–1958) quietly effective Vermont stories, collected in *In Four-Square* (1949), belong for the most part to an earlier period, as do Ben Ames Williams's (1889–1953) extremely competent and entertaining Maine stories, *Fraternity Village* (1949).[91] Donald Hall's *String Too Short To Be Saved* (1962) contains some moving and unpretentious reminiscences of boyhood on a New Hampshire

---

ment about "that slack tolerance or sentimental tenderness toward symptomatic evils that amounts to criminal collusion between author and character." (Introduction, *Selected Stories of Eudora Welty* [New York: Modern Library, 1954], pp. xx–xxi.)

[90] Farrell, like Saroyan, has been around so long, and continues to be so prolific, that one almost automatically tends to underestimate the importance of his total contribution. His relatively recent short story collections like *French Girls Are Vicious and Other Stories* (New York: Vanguard, 1955) are considerably more varied than and artistically superior to his early collections including *Calico Shoes* (1934) and *Guillotine Party* (1935).

[91] *In Four-Square* (New York: Harcourt, Brace, 1949) contains seventeen of Mrs. Fisher's best stories; *Fraternity Village* (Boston: Houghton Mifflin, 1949) contains sixteen of the approximately one hundred Fraternity Village stories, fifty-five of which were originally published in the *Saturday Evening Post*.

farm, and some of the best stories of Thomas Williams's (1926–) *A High New House* (1963) owe some of their effectiveness to a skillfully depicted New Hampshire setting. Among uncollected stories, far and away the best I have read is Lawrence Sargent Hall's (1915–) "The Ledge," a gripping, almost classic narrative of the destruction of a New England fisherman marooned with his son and nephew on a windswept, tide-threatened ledge.[92]

The essentially meaningful life of small town, rural community, or the country as opposed to the corrupting influence of metropolitan life is one of the most striking contrasts of much recent short fiction. In some stories, such as Oliver La Farge's "A Pause in the Desert" or Edward Loomis's "Mustangs," this contrast is specifically, almost didactically, spelled out; for the most part, such contrast is implicit in situation and character. This is not to suggest that the story set in small town, prairie, desert, hill or mountain country presents a rose-tinted picture of contemporary life. Quite the contrary. Tragedy and violence are as much a part of Eudora Welty's Mississippi as they are of Farrell's Chicago, but the deathly sickness of modern metropolitan life, which has engrossed so many major fiction writers since Joyce, has little counterpart in the writers who have fled or never lived in the New Yorks, Trentons, and Chicagos of America. The fiction of many of the big-city writers is essentially joyless; it tends to depict life as primarily meaningless, degrading, or both. Farrell's harlots, for example, drag their creaking bones wearily along dimly lit streets; sensitive youths dream in boyhood and are disillusioned in manhood; love turns to

[92] Originally published in the *Hudson Review*, "The Ledge" is the first-prize winner in the 1960 *Prize Stories*, ed. Mary Stegner, (New York: Doubleday, 1960).

ashes and hope to gloom, and the individual disintegrates
in an atmosphere of spiritual poverty and economic injustice.
Or, as it is depicted by some of the most extreme metropolitan Jeremiahs such as Leslie Fiedler, life itself has become
a suppurating wound or an insult. By contrast, the work of
writers like Saroyan or Faulkner or Clayton is full of fresh
air and sunlight, quick with the challenge of life, whether
that challenge end in triumph, disaster, or compromise. In
the final analysis, such writers present a much more varied
and, it seems to me, a more realistic, indeed truer, picture of
life than do their big city cousins. The feeling for place, the
love of the land which gives a sense of permanence to life
even in a dark age, is not rhetoric or boozy sentimentality or
escapism. Utterly anachronistic or unthinkable in the work
of an Albert Maltz, it is a living truth in that of a Jesse Stuart:

> It is our land after all and you never hear one of us speak
> against it when we are away. We tell you that it is our land,
> that we are a part of it . . . the good clean wind of a Ken-
> tucky spring . . . the silking corn and . . . the cries of the
> wild birds . . . and we show you that we cannot escape it
> no matter how cruel or how kind it has been to us. How can
> we be contented among a multitude of strangers and many
> tongues? [93]

[93] Jesse Stuart, "Plowshare in Heaven," *Plowshare in Heaven* (New
York: McGraw-Hill, 1958), pp. 271–72.

Story collections deeply concerned with places other than American
include Christine Weston's (1904–) excellent *There and Then; Stories of India* (New York: Scribner, 1947); John Berry's (1915–)
Flight of White Crows (New York: Macmillan, 1961), stories, tales,
and the unclassifiable "Pious Puzzles of Ananda Mahadev," all but
one of which are set in India; Pearl Buck's (1892–) uneven *Far and
Near; Stories of Japan, China, and America* (1947) and *Fourteen
Stories* (1961), both published by John Day, New York; Eugene
Burdick's (1918–) *The Blue of Capricorn* (Boston: Houghton Mifflin,
1961), a collection of stories and essays about people and places in

IV. *Spaceships, Aliens, and Bug-eyed Monsters*

What some of its recent admirers have termed the Golden Age of science fiction began somewhere around 1940, for reasons which apparently even the experts are hard put to explain, although World War II unquestionably seems to have primed the pump.[94] When almost every American family was in one way or another affected by the War, science fiction offered a ready avenue of escape from worry, stress, and tensions. At the same time, science fiction's blending of startling adventures and scientific or pseudo-scientific materials helped to satisfy a reading public whose appetites were being stimulated by daily newspaper and radio reports of almost unbelievable advances in science and technology.

Whatever the reasons for its rebirth, the short story of

---

the Pacific, as much ethnological, historical, and anthropological as fictional, as is James Michener's *Return to Paradise* (New York: Random House, 1951); and Robin White's excellent *Foreign Soil; Tales of South India* (New York: Atheneum, 1962). The most important single collection, if Massachusetts-born Mary Lavin can be included among American writers, is her *Selected Stories* (New York: Macmillan, 1959), chosen from Mrs. Lavin's six previous volumes of stories of Ireland where she has lived since her childhood.

[94] The best study of recent science fiction is Kingsley Amis's *New Maps of Hell; A Survey of Science Fiction* (New York: Harcourt, Brace, 1960). Amis, incidently, thinks that the War had relatively little to do with the science-fiction explosion.

science fiction and its often degenerate cousin fantasy,[95] is
one of the most controversial fictional forms of recent years,
a genre which almost inevitably evokes strongly partisan
opinions. To criticize s.f. adversely is to elicit cries of "snob"
or "square" from the faithful; to profess to admire it is to
provoke head-shakings among the intellectuals and cautious
suggestion that it is high time for you to seek the help of a
competent psychoanalyst. Each extreme is unsound and
unknowledgeable. The science fiction of the last twenty
years is not the treasure house created by master spirits that
some of its admirers claim it to be.[96] Neither, however, is it
the sub-literature that some of its critics have labeled it,
misled, perhaps, by the sloppy format, trashy covers, and in-
fantile advertisements which characterize even the best of
the science-fiction magazines.[97]

Following the era of the Great Pioneers, Jules Verne and
H. G. Wells, and the brief revival of the twenties, highlighted by the founding of *Weird Tales* and *Amazing Stories,*
science fiction rapidly deteriorated both in quantity and
quality. By the closing years of the thirties, there were only
five science-fiction magazines in America—as contrasted to
twenty-two three years later—and even the most dedicated
admirers of spaceships, moon maids, and mad scientists were
forced to admit that s.f. had become a combination of "sci-

[95] The terms, of course, should not be confused. Science fiction attempts to make the implausible or the impossible seem scientifically
accurate or, at the least, momentarily convincing. The writer of fantasy makes no such attempt to achieve verisimilitude, but, as Amis
comments, ignores or deliberately flouts fact (*op. cit.,* p. 22).
[96] See, for example, Raymond J. Healy and J. Francis McComas, Introduction, *Famous Science-Fiction Stories* (New York: Modern
Library, 1957), pp. xi–xvi.
[97] Those who know include *Galaxy Science Fiction, The Magazine of
Fantasy and Science Fiction, Astounding Stories,* and *Amazing
Stories.*

ence that was claptrap and fiction that was graceless and dull." [98]

After these doldrums, however, more and more writers of ability, and in some cases genuine talent, turned to science fiction. My own favorites—based on a small sampling of some three or four hundred recent s.f. stories, a mere drop in the bucket when one reflects that the big names in science fiction are alarmingly prolific—include, as might be expected, Ray Bradbury (1920–), the best known of all American writers in the field and, as far as I know, the only one to receive anything which approximates serious critical attention. Bradbury seems to me far and away the most consistently entertaining performer in the field, a formidable craftsman with a quick, alert mind and a sense of drama. Even Bradbury's less successful stories are for the most part free of the stylistic infelicities, the pseudo-scientific or pseudo-technological jargon, and the stereotyped characters and situations of so much recent science fiction. Among the others Isaac Asimov (1920–) seems both the most engaging and the most literate; like his British counterpart Arthur C. Clarke (1917–) and like Bradbury, Asimov not only tells an engaging, frequently arresting story, but for the most part tells it well. Again like Clarke, he is a man of standing in his own professional field—he is a biochemist in the Boston University School of Medicine—and perhaps because of this his stories are not overburdened or clogged with the pseudo-scientific-technological-sociological-historical flubdub and flummery which is the hallmark of much second-rate s.f.

Then there are Robert Heinlein (1907–), considered by some the "greatest of the giants," [99] whether writing under his own name or his pseudonym, Anson MacDonald; Robert Sheckley (1928–), s.f.'s "premier gadfly"; Frederik Pohl

[98] Healy and McComas, *op. cit.*, p. xi.
[99] *Ibid.*, xii.

(1919–) who has been labeled the "most consistently able" recent writer of science fiction in America, and Clifford Simak (1904–), a "kind of science-fiction poet laureate of the countryside."[100] Richard Matheson (1926–) is a versatile performer and author of what seems to me the best recent American novel in the field, *I Am Legend;* he, Cyril Kornbluth (1923–1958), James Blish, Fredric Brown (1906–), and, more recently, Avram Davidson, possess individual talent which set them apart, as I read them, from the mass.

Although these and other writers of science fiction have either been neglected or ignored or belittled for the wrong reasons, science fiction is still in its infancy. In spite of his laments that his markets are drying up, or his groans at not receiving his just acclaim, the writer of science fiction has really, it seems to me, had things pretty good during the last few years. But like the blind dog let loose in the butcher's shop, he has tried to gobble up too much too quickly, and in his own greediness has often perverted or debased what is potentially one of the most challenging and exciting literary forms of our times. The virtues inherent in s.f. are as conspicuous as the weaknesses of many of its practitioners, but for the most part s.f.'s shortcomings have been more widely commented upon than its strengths. One hardly need mention that the science fiction of yesterday has proved to be today's science; it seems logical to assume that this will continue, and that some of today's science fiction is likely to be tomorrow's science. Quite apart from his sometimes almost uncanny prophecies or lucky guesses, the writer of s.f. possesses other palpable assets, not the least of which is the fact that he is usually a cunning artisan who tells an engrossing story which quickly captures and usually maintains reader interest; his concerns are large, his subjects and

[100] Amis, *op. cit.,* pp. 116, 118, 74.

themes often variations of universal or archetypal fictional materials. Space travel, for example, until recently probably the most popular and most frequently written about science-fiction subject, has fascinated mankind since the Greeks. Similarly universal is the concept of the inspired, mad, or eccentric scientist or intellectual—Prometheus, Prospero, Faust—who with his beautiful daughter or fiancée or lab assistant appears and reappears in the s.f. or fantasy stories of the period. Equally "appealing" are stories of the menace of "aliens"—the trade term for any reasoning individual or creature originating beyond the earth—or stories of cataclysmic threats to mankind in the form of monsters —B-E-M's (bug-eyed monsters)—or changes in the earth precipitated by menace from without or overzealous scientific experimentation from within. These and other favorite s.f. subjects and themes are in many ways the contemporary offspring of such diverse literary ancestors as the epic (one thinks, for example, of *Beowulf* with its own brand of bug-eyed monsters, Grendel and his mother) or the fairy tale with its preoccupation with the grotesque, the horrible, and the supernatural. Such materials, so central to science fiction, apparently will continue to appeal to any generation of readers able and willing to indulge, with Coleridge, in the luxurious necessity of the willing suspension of disbelief.

One hardly need add that some of the progenitors of today's science fiction have found in the fantastic tale or the scientific spoof a vehicle for the most serious satire. Perhaps no body of contemporary literature is more concerned with the moral and practical dangers of overgrown technology than is science fiction. In the hide of an age in which technological progress has first overshadowed and ultimately threatened to engulf or destroy the individual, science fiction has been an angrily buzzing wasp. At its best, s.f.'s wide-

eyed interest and often uncritical admiration for the scientist are capable of being illuminated by a genuine concern
for individual man and the dangers which confront him
when "progress" becomes more important than reason.

On the other hand, in spite of its potentialities, science
fiction in recent years has tended to stumble as much as it
has walked. Its most appalling defect, it seems to me, is its
almost total lack of characterization. With very few exceptions, s.f.'s people, from the subhuman Yahoos of a
story like Avram Davidson's "Now Let Us Sleep" to the hate-
maddened monster of A. E. Van Vogt's (1912–) "Black De-
stroyer" or the Chief of the Bureau of Robotics of Asimov's
"Let's Get Together," are one-dimensional, lacking in individuality, almost completely devoid of complexity or even
the illusion of complexity. Like the villains, heroes, and
heroines of the old pulp Westerns, they exist on the surface
only. Lacking depth and breadth, they tend to lack reality;
lacking reality, they tend to fail to interest the adult reader,
regardless of the author's ingenuity or the potential meaningfulness of his ideas.

Almost equally distressing is the preponderance of what
can only be labeled the bad writing of much science fiction:
slovenly writing, trite writing, stereotyped writing, florid
writing overburdened with glittering adjectives and screaming adverbs. The frequently boozy or oversimplified metaphysics of science fiction, and its often labored passages of
pseudo-science, pseudo-history, and pseudo-economics are,
in my opinion, far less reprehensible than this sophomoric
writing. It remains to be seen whether the run-of-the-mill
science-fiction writer will continue, as Kingsley Amis has observed, to present "interesting ideas, and sometimes even
original ones, in terms of electrifying banality." [101] The
achievement of some of the writers I have mentioned here,

[101] *Ibid.*, p. 84.

writers who can be said to constitute the first important generation of science-fiction writers in America, suggests that though there will probably always be a hack on the periphery of s.f. the genre will attract more and more talented writers in the future than it has in the past. Certainly the achievement of such novels as *Brave New World, Childhood's End,* and *Lord of the Flies* indicates the possibilities inherent in the form.

7. Some Concluding Remarks

IN THE PRECEDING chapters I have tried to indicate what
seem to me the major directions and achievements of the
American short story since around the beginnings of World
War II. The quantity and diversity of American short fiction
in these years have frequently forced me to make some arbitrary classifications which I wish I could have avoided;
Louis Auchincloss or Jean Stafford, for example, might have
been included in Chapter Four, "Jane Austens of Metropolis
and Suburbia," rather than in Chapter Five, "Sick in Mind
and Body Both," or in both chapters. As much as possible,
I have tried to eliminate over-rigid or over-complex methods

of classification. At the same time, whenever possible I have avoided commenting on the same author in more than one chapter unless the varied nature of his work forces me to do so, as it does, for example, with the stories of Irwin Shaw, or J. D. Salinger.

The authors discussed or commented on in these pages have worked with admirable variety and artistry. With only a few exceptions they have been recognized by a small number of authors and critics, but for the most part have been ignored by the general book-buying public. In recent years, however, the short story writer has gradually emerged from this comparative oblivion. The old publishing taboo against collections of stories by individual authors has been broken so often as to no longer pose a threat; more and more collections of good short stories are being published, and occasional volumes of short fiction have achieved considerable popularity or recognition or both. Malamud's *The Magic Barrel* and Roth's *Goodbye, Columbus,* for example, were National Book Awards winners, and Salinger's *Franny and Zooey* and *Raise High the Roof Beam, Carpenters* were longtime best sellers.

Vigor, variety, and high artistic achievement, these seem to me to be the hallmarks of the recent short story in America. Whether the short story is the most important native literary contribution of the last two decades is something for subsequent literary historians and critics to assess; it seems to me that it is. Meanwhile, this study will more than serve its author's purpose if it leads new readers to some richly endowed and varied fiction writers who have quietly helped produce what seems to me the most exciting literary achievement of recent years.

What directions will the short story of the sixties take? Will the high achievements of the immediate past be equaled or surpassed? Who will the new short story writers be? Obviously, such questions cannot be answered, but it seems reasonable to assume that the short story will continue to flourish rather than wither. It will become even more flexible, I believe, and more varied than it currently is. It will continue to attract the young writer and challenge the resources of the established professional.[1] In two particular areas—the fields of science fiction and short stories by and about American Negroes—it seems likely that the form will move from the area of competent journalism to art. The short story will continue, it seems to me, to be the most challenging and vital of contemporary literary genres as well as the type most suited to the spirit and temper of our times.

The short story writers discussed in the preceding pages have much in common. James Purdy, John Cheever, and

[1] Among the "first" volumes which were published after this study was completed are Joyce Carol Oates's *By the North Gate* and Cecil Dawkins's *The Quiet Enemy;* first collections of short stories by young or new authors who have previously published a novel include Ellen Douglas's *Black Cloud, White Cloud* and Bruce Jay Friedman's *Far from the City of Class;* among the veterans, Bernard Malamud, John O'Hara, and Peter Taylor also published new volumes of short stories late in 1963. The variety of such collections suggests once again the largeness and flexibility of the contemporary short story. *By the North Gate,* one of the more impressive "first" books of 1963, is for the most part concerned with rural characters in western New York State; *The Quiet Enemy* ranges in setting from the Deep South to the Southwest and, like *By the North Gate,* is highlighted by insight, unassuming artistry, scenes of violence, a fondness for the grotesque. *Black Cloud, White Cloud,* two novellas and two short stories by the prizewinning author of *A Family's Affairs,* depicts white and Negro relations in the Mississippi towns of Philippi and Homochitto, and is primarily concerned with the interacting problems and effects of racial intolerance, misunderstanding and guilt. *Far from the City of Class,* by a native New Yorker, includes stories of contemporary Jews in America, viewed with understanding and occasional distaste.

Eudora Welty, for all their differences, possess the same interest in the problems of human loneliness, separateness, and unknowableness; and Truman Capote, Carson McCullers, and I. B. Singer are alike in their concern with the contrast between the real and the illusory, and in the hallucinated, dreamlike quality which makes their work so memorable. The search for self, the quest for understanding, the striving for meaning in a confused world—these and similar themes occur again and again in the short stories of the last two decades. In spite of remarkable variety of mood, method, and subject matter, at the center of this body of literature is twentieth-century man, whose problems differ in the final analysis only in degree, not in kind, from those of his predecessors. The short fiction of the last twenty years reminds us anew, if reminding is necessary, of the validity of Goethe's observation:

> *If you inquire what the people*
> *are like here, I must answer*
> *'The same as everywhere!'*

Appendix. One Hundred Notable American Short Story Writers, 1940–1963: A Checklist

I have included in this checklist a few authors like Conrad Aiken or William March or Wilbur Daniel Steele whose collected or selected stories were first published between 1940 and 1963 even though their major short fiction belongs primarily or wholly to the period prior to 1940. I have also listed a few authors, including Katherine Anne Porter and Ruth Suckow, whose major contribution to the field occurred before 1940 but who published individual volumes of short stories between 1940 and 1963. In such cases I have provided brief bibliographical notes. I have not included: "samplers" or specialized collections of previously published stories like *The Faulkner Reader* or Faulkner's *Big Woods*, reprints of selected or collected volumes originally published prior to 1940, like Hemingway's *The Fifth Column and the First Forty-Nine Stories*, or anthologies. Although the major emphasis is on what

I consider the importance of the authors listed, I have also tried to indicate the variety of the short fiction of the period. In a few cases birthdates have not been available.

AIKEN, CONRAD (1889–). *Collected Short Stories*. Cleveland: World, 1960.
This contains forty-one of Aiken's stories, several previously uncollected pieces and some pieces from his previous collections: *Bring! Bring! and Other Stories* (New York: Boni & Liveright, 1925), *Costumes by Eros* (New York: Scribner, 1928), and *Among the Lost People* (New York: Scribner, 1934). An earlier collected edition, *The Short Stories of Conrad Aiken*, was published by Duell, Sloan and Pearce in 1940.

ALGREN, NELSON (1909–). *The Neon Wilderness*. New York: Doubleday, 1948.

ANGOFF, CHARLES (1902–). *When I Was a Boy in Boston*. Boston: Beechhurst Press, 1947. *Something About My Father and Other People*. New York: Yoseloff, 1956.

AUCHINCLOSS, LOUIS (1917–). *The Injustice Collectors*. Boston: Houghton Mifflin, 1950. *The Romantic Egoists; A Reflection in Eight Minutes*. Boston: Houghton Mifflin, 1954. *Powers of Attorney*. Boston: Houghton Mifflin, 1963.
The Romantic Egoists is classified as a novel, but is a group of short stories with a central character and unifying theme. Five of the eight "chapters" appeared originally in such magazines as *The New Yorker, Harper's,* and *Harper's Bazaar;* two of the remaining three were originally published in *New World Writing*.

BECK, WARREN. *The Blue Sash and Other Stories*. Yellow Springs, Ohio: Antioch Press, 1941. *The First Fish and Other Stories*. Yellow Springs, Ohio: Antioch Press, 1947. *The Far Whistle and Other Stories*. Yellow Springs, Ohio: Antioch Press, 1951. *The Rest Is Silence and Other Stories*. Denver: Alan Swallow, 1963.

BEER, THOMAS (1888–1940). *Mrs. Egg and Other Americans; Collected Stories*. Wilson Follett, ed. New York: Knopf, 1947.

This is the first and thus far the last volume of a projected complete edition of the more than 150 stories Thomas Beer published during his lifetime; it consists of twenty-nine stories, three of which were previously unpublished. Only one volume of Beer's stories appeared during his lifetime, *Mrs. Egg and Other Barbarians* (New York: Knopf, 1933).

BEMELMANS, LUDWIG (1898–1962). *I Love You, I Love You, I Love You.* New York: Viking, 1942. *Hotel Bemelmans.* New York: Viking, 1946.

BENÉT, STEPHEN VINCENT (1898–1943). *Twenty-Five Short Stories.* New York: Doubleday, 1943. *The Last Circle.* New York: Farrar & Rinehart, 1946.

Twenty-Five Short Stories contains stories from Benét's previous collections, *Thirteen O'Clock; Stories of Several Worlds* (New York: Farrar & Rinehart, 1937) and *Tales Before Midnight* (New York: Farrar & Rinehart, 1939). *The Last Circle* contains fifteen stories and several poems, most of them written during Benét's last years.

BERKMAN, SYLVIA. *Blackberry Wilderness.* New York: Doubleday, 1959.

BETTS, DORIS. *The Gentle Insurrection and Other Stories.* New York: Putnam, 1954.

BOWLES, PAUL (1911–). *The Delicate Prey and Other Stories.* New York: Random House, 1950. *A Hundred Camels in the Courtyard.* San Francisco: City Lights Press, 1962.

BOYLE, KAY (1903–). *Thirty Stories.* New York: Simon & Schuster, 1946. *The Smoking Mountain; Stories of Postwar Germany.* New York: McGraw-Hill, 1951.

Thirty Stories contains stories from Miss Boyle's previous collections—*Wedding Day and Other Stories* (New York: Cape & Smith, 1930), *The First Lover and Other Stories* (New York: Smith and Haas, 1933), and *The White Horses of Vienna and Other Stories* (New York: Harcourt, Brace, 1936)—along with previously uncollected stories, including thirteen published in or after 1940.

BRADBURY, RAY (1920–). *The Martian Chronicles.* New York. Doubleday, 1950. *The Illustrated Man.* New York: Doubleday, 1951. *The Golden Apples of the Sun.* New York: Doubleday, 1953.

Fahrenheit 451. New York: Ballantine, 1953. *The October Country.* New York: Ballantine, 1955.

BRODKEY, HAROLD. *First Love and Other Sorrows.* New York: Dial, 1957.

BURNS, JOHN HORNE (1916–1953). *The Gallery.* New York: Harper, 1947.

CALDWELL, ERSKINE (1903–). *Jackpot.* New York: Duell, Sloan & Pearce, 1940. *Men and Women; Twenty-Two Stories.* Carvel Collins, ed. Boston: Little, Brown, 1961.

Jackpot contains seventy-five stories, nine of them hitherto uncollected, from Caldwell's several previous volumes including *American Earth* (New York: Scribner, 1931) and *We Are the Living* (1933), *Kneel to the Rising Sun and Other Stories* (1935), and *Southways* (1938), all published by Viking. *Erskine Caldwell's Men and Women* contains twenty-one stories selected from Caldwell's some hundred and fifty, chronologically arranged from childhood to death.

CALISHER, HORTENSE (1911–). *In the Absence of Angels.* Boston: Little, Brown, 1951. *Tale for the Mirror; A Novella and Other Stories.* Boston: Little, Brown, 1962.

CAPOTE, TRUMAN (1924–). *A Tree of Night and Other Stories.* New York: Random House, 1949. *Breakfast at Tiffany's; A Short Novel and Three Stories.* New York: Random House, 1958.

CHEEVER, JOHN (1912–). *The Way Some People Live; A Book of Stories.* New York: Random House, 1943. *The Enormous Radio and Other Stories.* New York: Funk & Wagnalls, 1953. *The Housebreaker of Shady Hill and Other Stories.* New York: Harper, 1958. *Some People, Places, and Things That Will Not Appear in My Next Novel.* New York: Harper, 1961. Four hitherto uncollected stories by Cheever are included in *Stories: Jean Stafford, John Cheever, Daniel Fuchs, William Maxwell* (New York: Farrar, Straus & Cudahy, 1956).

CLARK, WALTER VANTILBURG (1909–). *The Watchful Gods and Other Stories.* New York: Random House, 1950.

CLAYTON, JOHN BELL (1906–1955). *The Strangers Were There; Selected Stories.* New York: Macmillan, 1957.

COATES, ROBERT M. (1897–). *All the Year Round; A Book of Stories.* New York: Harcourt, Brace, 1943. *The Hour After Westerly and Other Stories.* New York: Harcourt, Brace, 1957.

DORRANCE, WARD (1904–). *The White Hound; Stories by Ward Dor-*

rance and Thomas Mabry. Columbia: Univ. of Missouri Press, 1959.

ELLIOTT, GEORGE P. *Among the Dangs.* New York: Holt, Rinehart, and Winston, 1961.

ENRIGHT, ELIZABETH (1909–). *Borrowed Summer and Other Stories.* New York: Rinehart, 1946. *The Moment Before the Rain.* New York: Harcourt, Brace, 1955. *The Riddle of the Fly and Other Stories.* New York: Harcourt, Brace, 1959.

FARRELL, JAMES T. (1904–). *When Boyhood Dreams Come True.* New York: Vanguard, 1946. *The Life Adventurous and Other Stories.* New York: Vanguard, 1947. *French Girls Are Vicious and Other Stories.* New York: Vanguard, 1955. *A Dangerous Woman and Other Stories.* New York: Vanguard, 1957.

Earlier volumes of Farrell's stories include *Calico Shoes and Other Stories* (1934), *Guillotine Party and Other Stories* (1935), and *Can All This Grandeur Perish and Other Stories* (1937), all published by Vanguard.

FAULKNER, WILLIAM (1897–1962). *Go Down, Moses and Other Stories.* New York: Random House, 1942. *Knight's Gambit.* New York: Random House, 1949. *Collected Stories.* New York: Random House, 1950.

In addition to previously uncollected Faulkner stories, the latter contains stories from *These Thirteen* (New York: Cape & Smith, 1931), *Doctor Martino and Other Stories* (New York: Smith & Haas, 1934), and *Go Down, Moses and Other Stories.*

FISHER, DOROTHY CANFIELD (1879–1958). *In Four-Square.* New York: Harcourt, Brace, 1949.

In Four-Square contains seventeen of Mrs. Fisher's best stories, most of them originally published prior to 1940.

FISHER, VARDIS (1895–). *Love and Death; Complete Stories.* New York: Doubleday, 1959.

GALLANT, MAVIS. *The Other Paris.* Boston: Houghton Mifflin, 1956.

GALLICO, PAUL (1897–). *Confessions of a Story Writer.* New York: Knopf, 1946. *Further Confessions of a Story Writer; Stories Old and New.* New York: Doubleday, 1961.

GARRETT, GEORGE (1929–). *King of the Mountain.* New York: Scribner, 1957. *In the Briar Patch; A Book of Stories.* Austin: Univ. of Texas Press, 1961. *Cold Ground Was My Bed Last Night.* Columbia: Univ. of Missouri Press, 1964.

GELLHORN, MARTHA (1908–). *The Honeyed Peace.* New York:

Doubleday, 1953. *Two by Two*. New York: Simon & Schuster, 1958.

GOLD, HERBERT (1924–). *Love and Like*. New York: Dial, 1960.

GORDON, CAROLINE (1895–). *The Forest of the South*. New York: Scribner, 1945. *Old Red and Other Stories*. New York: Scribner, 1963.

GOYEN, WILLIAM (1915–). *Ghost and Flesh; Stories and Tales*. New York: Random House, 1952. *The Faces of Blood Kindred; A Novella and Ten Stories*. New York: Random House, 1960.

GRAU, SHIRLEY ANN (1929–). *The Black Prince and Other Stories*. New York: Knopf, 1954.

HALE, NANCY (1908–). *Between the Dark and the Daylight*. New York: Scribner, 1943. *The Empress's Ring*. New York: Scribner, 1955. *Heaven and Hardpan Farm*. New York: Scribner, 1957. *A New England Girlhood*. Boston: Little, Brown, 1958. *The Pattern of Perfection*. Boston: Little, Brown, 1960.
Miss Hale's earliest collection is *The Earliest Dreams* (New York: Scribner, 1936).

HUGHES, LANGSTON (1902–). *Laughing to Keep from Crying*. New York: Holt, 1952.
Hughes's earliest collection is *The Ways of White Folks* (New York: Knopf, 1934).

HUMPHREY, WILLIAM (1925–). *The Last Husband and Other Stories*. New York: Morrow, 1953.

JACKSON, CHARLES (1903–). *The Sunnier Side; Twelve Arcadian Tales*. New York: Farrar, Straus, 1950. *Earthly Creatures; Ten Stories*. New York: Farrar, Straus & Young, 1953.

JACKSON, SHIRLEY (1919–). *The Lottery, or the Adventures of James Harris*. New York: Farrar, Straus, 1949.

KENTFIELD, CALVIN (1925–). *The Angel and the Sailor; A Novella and Nine Stories*. New York: McGraw-Hill, 1957. *The Great Wondering Goony Bird*. New York: Random House, 1963.

LA FARGE, CHRISTOPHER (1897–1956). *The Wilsons*. New York: Coward-McCann, 1941. *East by Southwest*. New York: Coward-McCann, 1944. *All Sorts and Kinds*. New York: Coward-McCann, 1949.

LA FARGE, OLIVER (1901–1963). *A Pause in the Desert; A Collection of Short Stories*. Boston: Houghton Mifflin, 1957.
La Farge has an earlier collection, *All the Young Men* (Boston: Houghton Mifflin, 1935).

LOWRY, ROBERT (1919–). *The Wolf that Fed Us.* New York: Doubleday, 1949. *Happy New Year, Kamerades!* New York: Doubleday, 1954. *The Last Party.* New York: Popular Library, 1956. *New York Call Girl.* New York: Doubleday, 1958. *Party of Dreamers.* New York: Fleet, 1962.

LYTLE, ANDREW (1902–). *A Novel, a Novella, and Four Stories.* New York: McDowell, Obolensky, 1958.

MABRY, THOMAS (1903–). *See* Dorrance, Ward.

McCARTHY, MARY (1912–). *The Company She Keeps.* New York: Simon & Schuster, 1942. *Cast a Cold Eye.* New York: Harcourt, Brace, 1950.

MACAULEY, ROBIE (1919–). *The End of Pity and Other Stories.* New York: McDowell, Obolensky, 1957.

McCULLERS, CARSON (1917–). *The Ballad of the Sad Cafe.* Boston: Houghton Mifflin, 1951.

McNULTY, JOHN (1895–1956). *The World of John McNulty.* New York: Doubleday, 1957.
   The World of John McNulty contains stories from *Third Avenue, New York* (Boston: Little, Brown, 1946), *A Man Gets Around* (Boston: Little, Brown, 1951), *My Son Johnny* (New York: Simon & Schuster, 1955), and twenty previously uncollected stories.

MALAMUD, BERNARD (1914–). *The Magic Barrel.* New York: Farrar, Straus & Cudahy, 1958. *Idiots First.* New York: Farrar, Straus, 1963.

MARCH, WILLIAM (1893–1954). *Trial Balance; Collected Short Stories.* New York: Harcourt, Brace, 1945.
   Trial Balance contains stories from *The Little Wife and Other Stories* (New York: Harrison Smith, 1935), *Some Like Them Short* (Boston: Little, Brown, 1939), and ten uncollected stories published after 1940.

MARSHALL, PAULE (1929–). *Soul Clap Hands and Sing.* New York: Atheneum, 1961.

MICHENER, JAMES A. (1907–). *Tales of the South Pacific.* New York: Macmillan, 1947. *Return to Paradise.* New York: Random House, 1951.

MITCHELL, JOSEPH (1908–). *McSorley's Wonderful Saloon.* New York: Duell, Sloan & Pearce, 1943.

NABOKOV, VLADIMIR (1899–). *Nine Stories.* Norfolk, Conn.: New Directions, 1947. *Nabokov's Dozen.* New York: Doubleday, 1958.

NEWHOUSE, EDWARD (1911–). *Anything Can Happen.* New York: Harcourt, Brace, 1941. *The Iron Chain.* New York: Harcourt, Brace, 1946. *Many Are Called; Forty-Two Short Stories.* New York: Sloane, 1951.

O'CONNOR, FLANNERY (1925–). *A Good Man Is Hard to Find and Other Stories.* New York: Harcourt, Brace, 1955.

O'HARA, JOHN (1905–). *Pal Joey.* New York: Duell, Sloan & Pearce, 1940. *Pipe Night.* New York: Duell, Sloan & Pearce, 1945. *Hellbox.* New York: Random House, 1947. *Assembly.* New York: Random House, 1961. *The Cape Cod Lighter.* New York: Random House, 1962. *The Hat on the Bed.* New York: Random House, 1963.

O'Hara's previous volumes of short stories are *The Doctor's Son and Other Stories* (New York: Duell, Sloan & Pearce, 1935) and *Files on Parade* (New York: Harcourt, Brace, 1939).

OLSEN, TILLIE. *Tell Me a Riddle.* Philadelphia: Lippincott, 1961.

PALEY, GRACE. *The Little Disturbances of Man.* New York: Doubleday, 1959.

PORTER, KATHERINE ANNE (1890–). *The Leaning Tower and Other Stories.* New York: Harcourt, Brace, 1944.

Except for *The Leaning Tower,* Miss Porter's stories are essentially products of the twenties and thirties. *Flowering Judas* was first published in a limited edition in 1930 and in a trade edition, which included four additional stories, by Harcourt, Brace in 1935. *Pale Horse, Pale Rider,* a collection of three novellas one of which was originally published by itself, appeared in 1939, from Harcourt, Brace.

POWERS, J. F. (1917–). *Prince of Darkness.* New York: Doubleday, 1947. *The Presence of Grace.* New York: Doubleday, 1956.

PRICE, REYNOLDS (1933–). *The Names and Faces of Heroes.* New York: Atheneum, 1963.

PURDY, JAMES (1923–). *Color of Darkness; Eleven Stories and a Novella.* Norfolk, Conn.: New Directions, 1957. *Children Is All.* Norfolk, Conn.: New Directions, 1962.

RAWLINGS, MARJORIE KINNAN (1896–1953). *When the Whippoorwill—.* New York: Scribner, 1940.

ROSTEN, LEO [Leonard Q. Ross](1908–). *The Return of H*Y*M*A*N K*A*P*L*A*N.* New York: Harper, 1959.

Appendix

An earlier collection of Mr. Kaplan stories, *The Education of H*Y*M*A*N K*A*P*L*A*N,* was published in 1937 by Harcourt, Brace.

ROTH, PHILIP (1933–). *Goodbye, Columbus and Five Short Stories.* Boston: Houghton Mifflin, 1959.

SALINGER, J. D. (1919–). *Nine Stories.* Boston: Little, Brown, 1953. *Franny and Zooey.* Boston: Little, Brown, 1961. *Raise High the Roof Beam, Carpenters* and *Seymour—An Introduction.* Boston: Little, Brown, 1963.

SAROYAN, WILLIAM (1908–). *My Name Is Aram.* New York: Harcourt, Brace, 1940. *Dear Baby.* New York: Harcourt, Brace, 1945. *The Assyrian and Other Stories.* New York: Harcourt, Brace, 1950. *Love.* New York: Lion Books, 1955. *The Whole Voyald and Other Stories.* Boston: Little, Brown, 1956.

It was, of course, Saroyan's first book, *The Daring Young Man on the Flying Trapeze and Other Stories,* published by Random House in 1934, that made him a literary sensation overnight.

SCHORER, MARK (1908–). *The State of Mind.* Boston: Houghton Mifflin, 1947.

SCHWARTZ, DELMORE (1913–). *The World Is a Wedding.* Norfolk, Conn.: New Directions, 1948. *Successful Love and Other Stories.* New York: Corinth Books, 1961.

SEAGER, ALLAN (1906–). *The Old Man of the Mountain and Seventeen Other Stories.* New York: Simon & Schuster, 1950.

SHAW, IRWIN (1913–). *Welcome to the City and Other Stories.* New York: Random House, 1942. *Act of Faith and Other Stories.* New York: Random House, 1946. *Mixed Company; Collected Short Stories.* New York: Random House, 1950. *Tip on a Dead Jockey and Other Stories.* New York: Random House, 1957.

In addition to stories from *Welcome to the City* and *Act of Faith, Mixed Company* contains stories from Shaw's first volume, *Sailor off the Bremen and Other Stories* (Random House, 1939), plus seven previously uncollected stories and one hitherto unpublished story.

SINGER, ISAAC BASHEVIS (1904–). *Gimpel the Fool and Other Stories.* New York: Noonday, 1957. *The Spinoza of Market Street.* New York: Farrar, Straus & Cudahy, 1961.

STAFFORD, JEAN (1915–). *Children Are Bored on Sunday.* New York: Harcourt, Brace, 1953.

Four additional uncollected stories by Miss Stafford are included in *Stories: Jean Stafford, John Cheever, Daniel Fuchs, William Maxwell.*

STEELE, WILBUR DANIEL (1886–). *The Best Stories of Wilbur Daniel Steele.* New York: Doubleday, 1946. *Full Cargo; More Stories.* New York: Doubleday, 1951.

These collections are from stories originally published in *Land's End and Other Stories* (1918), *The Shame Dance and Other Stories* (1923), *The Man Who Saw Through Heaven and Other Stories* (1927), and *Tower of Sand and Other Stories* (1929), all published by Harper, and *Urkey Island* (1926), published by Harcourt, Brace.

STEGNER, WALLACE (1909–). *The Women on the Wall.* Boston: Houghton Mifflin, 1949. *The City of the Living.* Boston: Houghton Mifflin, 1956.

STILES, BERT (1920–1944). *Serenade to the Big Bird.* New York: Norton, 1952.

STUART, JESSE (1907–). *Men of the Mountain.* New York: Dutton, 1941. *Tales from the Plum Grove Hills.* New York: Dutton, 1946. *Clearing in the Sky and Other Stories.* New York: McGraw-Hill, 1950. *Plowshare in Heaven; Stories.* New York: McGraw-Hill, 1958.

Stuart's first volume of stories is *Head of W— Hollow* (New York: Dutton, 1936).

SUCKOW, RUTH (1892–1960). *Some Others and Myself; Seven Stories and a Memoir.* New York: Rinehart, 1952.

Miss Suckow's previous story collections include *Iowa Interiors* (New York: Knopf, 1926), *Children and Older People* (New York: Knopf, 1931), and *Carry-Over* (New York: Farrar & Rinehart, 1936).

TAYLOR, PETER (1917–). *A Long Fourth and Other Stories.* New York: Harcourt, Brace, 1948. *The Widows of Thornton.* New York: Harcourt, Brace, 1954. *Happy Families Are All Alike: A Collection of Stories.* New York: McDowell, Obolensky, 1959. *Miss Leonora When Last Seen & Fifteen Other Stories.* New York: Obolensky, 1963.

THURBER, JAMES (1894–1961). *My World—and Welcome to It.* New York: Harcourt, Brace, 1942. *The Thurber Carnival.* New York: Harper, 1945.

In addition to six previously uncollected pieces, *The Thurber Carnival* contains stories from *My Life and Hard Times* (1933), *The Middle-Aged Man on the Flying Trapeze; A Collection of Short Pieces* (1935), and *Let Your Mind Alone; and Other More or Less Inspirational Pieces* (1937), all published by Harper, and *My World—and Welcome to It*.

UPDIKE, JOHN (1932–). *The Same Door; Short Stories.* New York: Knopf, 1959. *Pigeon Feathers.* New York: Knopf, 1962.

VAN DOREN, MARK (1894–). *The Witch of Ramoth and Other Tales.* York, Penn.: Maple Press, 1950. *Short Stories of Mark Van Doren.* New York: Abelard, 1950. *Nobody Said a Word and Other Stories.* New York: Holt, 1953. *Home with Hazel and Other Stories.* New York: Harcourt, Brace, 1957. *Collected Stories.* New York: Hill & Wang, 1962.

WARREN, ROBERT PENN (1905–). *The Circus in the Attic and Other Stories.* New York: Harcourt, Brace, 1948.

WEIDMAN, JEROME (1913–). *The Captain's Tiger.* New York: Reynal & Hitchcock, 1947. *A Dime a Throw.* New York: Doubleday, 1957. *My Father Sits in the Dark and Other Selected Stories.* New York: Random House, 1961. *Back Talk.* New York: Random House, 1963.

WELTY, EUDORA (1909–). *A Curtain of Green.* New York: Harcourt, Brace, 1941. *The Wide Net.* New York: Harcourt, Brace, 1943. *The Golden Apples.* New York: Harcourt, Brace, 1949. *The Bride of the Innisfallen and Other Stories.* New York: Harcourt, Brace, 1955.

WEST, JESSAMYN (1907–). *The Friendly Persuasion.* New York: Harcourt, Brace, 1945. *Love, Death, and the Ladies' Drill Team.* New York: Harcourt, Brace, 1955.

WESTON, CHRISTINE (1904–). *There and Then; Stories of India.* New York: Scribner, 1947.

WHITE, ROBIN. *Foreign Soil; Tales of South India.* New York: Atheneum, 1962.

WILLIAMS, TENNESEE (1914–). *One Arm and Other Stories.* Norfolk, Conn.: New Directions, 1948, 1954. *Hard Candy; A Book of Stories.* Norfolk, Conn.: New Directions, 1954.

WILLIAMS, THOMAS. *A High New House.* New York: Dial, 1963.

WILLIAMS, WILLIAM CARLOS (1883–1963). *Make Light of It; Collected Stories.* New York: Random House, 1950.

Make Light of It contains stories from *The Knife of the Times* (Ithaca, New York: Dragon Press, 1932) and *Life Along the Passaic River* (New York: New Directions, 1938), together with twenty-one previously uncollected stories, thirteen of them published for the first time. *The Farmers' Daughters; The Collected Stories of William Carlos Williams* (Norfolk, Conn.: New Directions, 1961) is identical to *Make Light of It,* except for the long title piece and a brief introduction by Van Wyck Brooks.

WILSON, EDMOND (1895–). *Memoirs of Hecate County.* New York: Doubleday, 1946. Rev. ed.; New York: L. C. Page, 1959.

WINDHAM, DONALD. *The Warm Country.* New York: Scribner, 1962. *Emblems of Conduct.* New York: Scribner, 1963.

YATES, RICHARD (1926–). *Eleven Kinds of Loneliness.* Boston: Little, Brown, 1962.

YELLEN, SAMUEL (1906–). *The Passionate Shepherd; A Book of Stories.* New York: Knopf, 1957.

Index

NOTE: Books and stories are listed alphabetically under the names of their authors.